# THE DRONTHEIM

## Forgotten Sailing Boat of the North Irish Coast

A New and Enlarged Second Edition to Include the Boats of the North East Coast and Islay

*Dónal MacPolin*
*June 2000*

## Dónal MacPolin

With a Technical Description by Kevin McLaverty

*For Jim McFarlane*

# CONTENTS

FOREWORD   v

**THE DRONTHEIM**

The Drontheim Boat   1

How Did the Drontheim Come To Ireland?   5

The Boat and its Construction.   15

What Makes the Drontheim Unique?   20

The Builders   30

Life on the Drontheims   36

Fishing   49

**THE DRONTHEIM COMMUNITIES**

THE NORTH-WEST COAST

Donegal Bay   54

Teelin   60

Arranmore   62

Innishboffin and Tory   66

THE NORTH-EAST COAST   75

Portstewart and Portush   76

Dunseverick, Portbraddan and Ballintoy   82

RATHLIN AND ISLAY

Rathlin Island   91

Islay *"An Sgoth Eireannach"* - The Irish Skiff   101

**DISASTERS & CONCLUSION**

Disasters   116

Conclusion   121

**APPENDICES**

Technical Description of Greencastle Yawl   122

Glossary   135

List of Gaelic Terms   136

List of Scots-Gaelic Terms   137

A Word of Thanks   139

Boat and Sail-Plans   141

ISBN   0  9536380  0  6

# THE DRONTHEIM
Forgotten Sailing Boat of the North Irish Coast

Text and illustrations by Dónal MacPolin
Book design by Paul Rowe
Typeset in Adobe Garamond,Caflisch Script and Bodoni Poster
Printing and binding by PlayPrint Limited, 80 St. Ignatius Road, Dublin 7 Ireland, 1999

*Cover Illustration:*　　　Drontheim at the Malin Head Regatta. c.1920
　　　　　　　　　　*Crew:* Paddy 'John' Mc Daid, Big James Mc Daid, Paddy 'Barney' McGonagle
　　　　　　　　　　　　Mickey 'John Philip' Doherty and John 'Philip' Doherty.

This project has been supported by Inishowen Rural Development Ltd.
under the Leader II Programme

# FOREWORD

*The last wave on the seashore…*

*The old men are nearly all gone now. They lived in that time when the fisherman/farmer lived an uncertain precarious existence, subject to the whim of weather, landlord or fish-buyer, and to the primeval return of herring or salmon, when all boats were wood and power was sail or oar… part of age-old communities living on estuary, island or rocky coast.*

*Their memories are hazy now, the once-great arms frail, but eyes still flash with excitement as they recall great men on oar or sail, hardships endured, catches and famines…. they are incorrigible storytellers, rarely dealing in 'hard' facts. Information is wonderfully dispensed by way of story. Events and facts are remembered primarily as a vehicle to amuse or delight, not to record history. Events illustrate the times in which they lived, the people they knew, the great sights they saw. However, they retain little nostalgia for a life that was often hard and dangerous but had a quality that is missing today.*

*Their time is passing swiftly. Only a few boats remain now, making a fragile connection with the generations before who were born to oar, wood, and unimaginable hardship. So much is already forgotten. The skill to make the boats still survives, in younger hands now. A new generation is learning the old boat skills again. Of those who sailed the yawls to fish or race, Jim Mc Farlane of Islay alone still sails as he did with his grandfather and he knows the boats and their ways intimately. Inishboffin men too, such as Jimmy Ferry and Sean O'Brien are getting ready to sail their fathers' boats again.*

*When the first edition of this little book on the drontheims appeared in 1992 only one of the old boats had been sailed again, that of Bernard Barr of Moville. It has sailed every summer since. But now more are being restored and sailed, at Inishboffin, at Arranmore, and at Moville. The first new drontheim built for almost fifty years was built in 1996 and today sails from the isle of Islay in Scotland. Another was built at Moneygold in Sligo in 1997. Two more were built at Moville this year. A huge renewal of interest in the drontheim has taken place all over the north coast and their future is secure.*

*The greatest pleasure of all, apart from seeing drontheims sailing again, has been to meet the drontheim folk of the north east. I knew nothing of these men before 1992 when I thought the drontheim was solely a Donegal boat….Antrim men like Sammy Wilkinson of Ballintoy, Sammy Gault of Dunseverick, Bertie Mckay of the beautiful Portbraddan, Loughie McQuilkin of Rathlin, Jim McFarlane of Islay and many more, all fishermen in their youth and still full of stories of men and boats. Again I can only quote directly from them because I could never tell a story the way they can. They are the last witnesses to a life and a world that is gone forever.*

*They are now the last wave on the seashore.*

Dónal MacPolin. Moville, Co.Donegal March 1999

*v*

GREENCASTLE, CO. DONEGAL.

**Drontheims at Greencastle. c. 1900.**
**Baiting the Long Lines with Cuhorns (Whelks)**
(Courtesy Mr. & Mrs. M. Kelly)

# THE DRONTHEIM BOAT

Visitors to any of the local regattas held around the north coast of Ireland in the 1950s, at Moville or Arranmore, Portstewart or Rathlin, would have watched sailing and rowing races which featured a remarkably beautiful and graceful open boat referred to by the locals as a "yawl" or "skiff" but more often by the strange name of a 'Drontheim Boat'. They would not have realised that they were watching a boat whose origins stretched back to the great Viking ships of the 8th and 9th centuries. A secretary to the Royal Sea Fisheries Commission in 1866 describes seeing the boats in Moville :

*"The largest of these yawls is about 24ft. on the keel with a 6ft. beam, and they carry two sprit-sails and sometimes a jib. Good, well-shaped oars are used with them, and they row and sail well, although a little tender down to a certain point"* [1]

Today they have all but disappeared, as the men who sailed them and the life that they sustained has been replaced by the steel

**The Last Drontheim to Sail out of the Foyle  c. 1950s.**
The boat belonged to Charlie 'The Cat' McLaughlin of Moville

trawler and high technology fishing. In its day, however, the drontheim in the cold and stormy northern waters was unsurpassed in its ability to meet the fishing needs of the small communities it served from Donegal Bay and east to Ballycastle and Co. Down.

The drontheim would have resembled superficially many other boats of its day around Northern Europe but it had many distinctive and unique features. It was an open i.e. undecked boat, carrying from four to seven men. It could be quite

large - between 26 and 28 feet long. It was 'double-ended' i.e. the bow and stern were almost similar, and was 'clinker-built' i.e. the planks of her sides overlapped, as opposed to being fitted edge-to-edge as in a smooth-sided or 'carvel'-built boat.

*"With the carvel you just clad the boat with wood. With the clinker there is room for the poet"*
(Kevin McLaverty)

She carried either one or two 'sprit' sails and a jib. A 'sprit' being a long, loose thin pole which held the high

---

[1] Deep Sea Fishing and Fishing Boats.
E.W. Holdsworth. 1866

IRISH FISHING YAWL.

peak of the sail. This was held by a 'beckit' i.e. a double-looped piece of rope, one loop of which was around the mast, the other holding the foot of the sprit. She had a shallow keel and carried bags of gravel or large stones for ballast. If she was rowed she relied on the strength of her crew pulling great 16, 18 or even 21 ft oars. These latter being called 'great oars' or 'sweeps'. There were six thwarts or seats on the drontheim, referred to only as 'beams'. The fifth was loose so it could be removed to accommodate nets and other cargo. At Culmore, near Derry, this beam was called the 'waterroom-beam'.

The drontheim held sway over a great range of northern ocean for a great many generations, but is origins and history go back to a different age and place.

**Greencastle Yawl,** Moville, Co. Donegal, from an engraving by E.W.H. Holdsworth 1866
UF&TM L1087/2

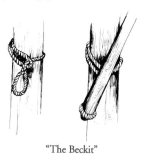

"The Beckit"

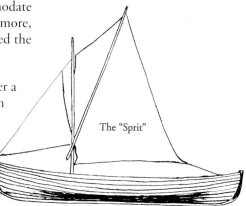

The "Sprit"

# THE DRONTHEIM

The name 'Drontheim' is a local name given to these craft and has a curious and ancient origin :

*"In Northern Ireland is to be found a craft known variously, according to her district as a Greencastle or Skerries yawl. Another name for her is 'Drontheim'. No more suggestive evidence need be given for her descent than these names; for 'yawl' is derived from the Norse 'YOL' used of a similar double-ended boat, and 'Drontheim' may be traced to a time when, about a hundred years ago, these boats were imported from Norway".[2]*

**Drontheims at Burtonport**
Co. Donegal c. 1930
Courtesy Mrs. Anne Loane, Enniskillen,
UF&TM L2297/8

"Drontheim" or "Drunton" was the colloquial pronunciation of Trondheim, or Trondhjem, the town in Norway from which many of the boats of this model were imported.

**"Just arrived to Abraham McCausland. Cargo of beft white and red Drunton Deal and a few half and a quarter barrels of Norway Tar"**
(DERRY JOURNAL 1772)

Drontheims were once built all round the north Irish coast.

Only the family of MacDonalds who once built drontheims in Greencastle are left. Today they still make wooden clinker-built boats in nearby Moville. Similar lines, grace and workmanship can been seen in the modern descendants of their drontheims now carrying diesel engines, net-haulers and the other paraphernalia of modern fishing.

Until the introduction of the internal combustion engine in the early 20th century brought design and constructional changes, this type of sailing and pulling boat was

[2] "Shipping Wonders of the World" Vol. 1 (London c.1937) P.1701
"Open Boats of the British Coasts".

**Dromtheims pulled up at Moville**
Co. Donegal c. 1920
(U. Mus. RW 1446)

MOVILLE, CO.DONEGAL. R.W. 1446.

the characteristic craft of the north, and north east coast of Ireland. The drontheim was the local variation especially suited to the northern coastline.

The Irish distribution of this boat type "formed part of a north-west European boat-building tradition, centred on Scandinavia, where there has been a continuity of the double-ended clinker-building technique for more than 1000 years!" [3]

[3] "Ulster Boat Types in Old Photographs" Michael McCaughan. Ulster Folklife. Vol. 28 1982

# HOW DID THE DRONTHEIM COME TO IRELAND?

There is no doubt that the drontheim, together with all clinker-built boats derived essentially from Scandinavia where this method of construction had evolved from the earliest times. Clinker-built boats first came to England, Scotland, and then Ireland with the Vikings in the 8th century. This method of building boats became established in Viking colonies in these countries, as the Viking communities passed on their skills to the natives. Evidence of early Irish clinker-built galleys dating from the 16th. century can be seen, for instance, in an old stone-carving of one in Dunluce Castle, Co. Antrim. It depicts a clinker-built galley, carved there

'Lord of the Isles' Galley
Built at McDonalds 1991

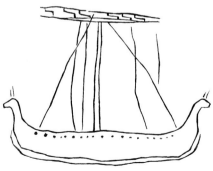

The Dunluce Galley

perhaps by a MacDonnell, cousin to the McDonalds of the Western Isles. It shows a substantial vessel, which was propelled by oars or sail and could be used for transporting trading goods or raiding parties of armed men, such raiding being a popular pastime in the 16th century! (In 1990 McDonalds of Moville built a replica of such a galley for the clan MacDonald of today). No doubt smaller clinker-built boats of similar size to the drontheim were built here as well but no significant archeological

remains of such boats has been uncovered in Ireland to date.

Carvel boats were more usual on the west coast along with the native *curragh*. At the turn of the century the clinker-built yawl replaced these old heavier 'wall-sided' boats and became the dominant fishing vessel of most of the north coast, though the *curragh* survived in Donegal alongside the drontheim to the present day. In South Mayo and Galway such change was resisted and the carvel tradition survives alongside the *curragh* there to this day.

**Norway Yawl at Portstewart,**
Co. Derry 1822. (from a painting by
J.W. Cambell) UF&TM L1689/8

As Ireland's timber resources became depleted by the middle of the 18th century, Norway became the main supplier of timber from its ports of Trondheim and Kristiansund in the north, and Bergen and Kristiansand in the south. With this trade a second colonisation of Scandinavian boats occurred. Along with timber and ice, trading vessels from Norway brought small clinker-built boats. These Norway yawls were carried as supplementary deck cargo for sale wherever the timber-ships dropped anchor.

A Letter from a Derry merchant to the master of a chartered ship Nedelven out of Trondheim, May 16th. 1828 read:

*"We have to request your attention in taking in the cargo that you will reject any coarse, knotty deals that should be sent you. Also, if you can bring in a few good drontheim boats they would pay you here."*

We have almost no evidence of what these early Irish yawls looked like, except for some vague local tradition, some 19th. century shipping references, old photographs, and illustrations such as the 1822 painting of a double ended, clinker boat at Portstewart.

There is some similarity between the Drontheim and the small vernacular boats of Norway in the last two centuries and for a clue as to their appearance we can look to Scotland. The trade in small craft from Norway is most likely to have begun with Shetland, where there was no timber at all, and eventually extended to the ports importing Baltic timber into Ireland, Derry, Belfast, Newry, Drogheda and Dublin. It is interesting to note that, where local timber for boatbuilding was non-existent such as in Shetland, the small craft there remain closest in appearance to the Norwegian small boats of the 20th century.

From the 9th to the 15th century the Orkney and Shetland islands were Norwegian territory. They were colonised by the Vikings as they spread west and south in their great longships. It is not surprising, therefore, that their ship-building style and methods were copied by the fishermen and boat-builders of these islands, linking them directly with the great Viking ships of Oseberg and Gokstad. These were two great long-ships built by the Vikings in the 9th century and which were found, almost intact, in Norway in the late 19th century. They mark the high point of ancient Norse boat technology. The techniques of their construction are uncannily similar to those of the drontheim and to the Orkney and Shetland boats of today.

The original boats brought to Shetland were not fully complete

when they came but were in the form of shaped boards and frames all ready to be erected. These "prefabricated boats" were then completed in Shetland from the kit of boards which

had come from Norway. This was easier and cheaper in a land without trees!

*"The boats from Norway were built with three boards a side and were very cheap, much cheaper than they could be built in Shetland. They were improved to suit the needs of the 'haaf' fishermen, being made deeper by the addition of a top strake."*

When timber could be brought in cheaply the Shetland builders improved on this older shape.

The Gokstad Ship 8th Century

[1] Edgar J. March "Inshore Craft of Britian in the Days of Sail and Oar" David & Charles: Newton Abbot. 1970 p. 43

Norwegian fjord boats were less suitable for the harsh fishing seas around Shetland and were modified and improved though as mentioned they remained much closer to the original Norwegian form and style than their Irish cousins were to do. Their shape is spoken of as 'The Shetland Model'.

The notable features of the Shetland model were flared topsides, few and wide planks with few frames, narrow at the waterline, low freeboard amidships, long and curved overhanging stem and stern, lug-sails and Norwegian-style oar locks. They were manned by four or six oarsmen and were consequently called *fourerns* (four-man boats), *sixerns* or *sixareens* (six-man boats).

The Shetland Fourern

Viking boat technology spread to all the areas they colonised. It remained largely unchanged to our day because it was wonderfully efficient and perfectly suited to the needs of fishermen till the coming of the diesel engine.

The Viking shipwright and the Irish drontheim builder would have understood each other very well! Basic design, tools, terminology, and construction have altered remarkably little between A.D. 900 and A.D. 1900, as we shall see.

When Viking influence spread to Ireland their superior boat technology advanced and in places replaced the primitive native tradition. The *curragh* still survived but through succeeding centuries the Viking ship technology dominated much of Western Scottish and Irish

Tools from McDonald's Boatyard, Moville

Viking Plane, Wood Quay, Dublin, 8th c.

boat-building on the north and east coasts.

## IRELAND AND THE NORSE BOATS

So, were the boats which came to Ireland in the 18th century similar to these Shetland ones, with their distinctive Norse characteristics? Most probably. Tradition and historical sources tell us the forebears of the drontheim came from Norway, but what shape and style were they? Old photographs of boats at Warrenpoint, Co. Down suggest a style but evidence is scant. Local tradition can tell us little. Sammy Wilkinson, a drontheim fisherman of Ballintoy who fished 22ft. drontheims said that he had heard that yawls came to Rathlin Island 400 years ago. This date may seem a little fanciful but

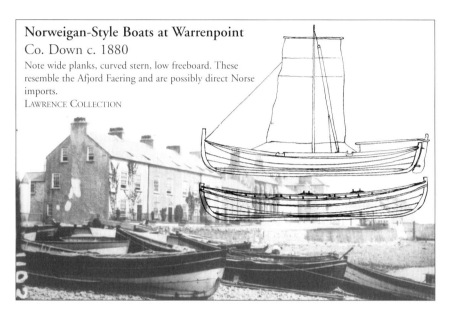

**Norweigan-Style Boats at Warrenpoint**
Co. Down c. 1880
Note wide planks, curved stern, low freeboard. These resemble the Afjord Faering and are possibly direct Norse imports.
LAWRENCE COLLECTION

he describes their evolution as he heard it:

*"The first boats I think, that came here were, you know, the ones with the high bow and stern. They came fe Norway. Well, then they gradually took that away. The local people got them built the same lines as these boats are now (here) ....... more suitable. A big high bow caught terrible wind. Nowadays, in these (modern) boats they "higher the board" as they talk about than what they were in the early days. But that's only hearsay, handed down, even my father, he never even remembered them boats."*

## LOCAL BUILDERS

As time passed Irish boat-builders began to copy the imported Norse boats and adapt them to their local needs and conditions, directed, no doubt, by the men who would fish them. This adaptation began as early as the 18th century when supplies of timber to Britain, Scotland, and Ireland were halted by the Napoleonic wars. Local boat-builders, in attempting to copy the Norwegian boats were also limited by the availability of timber. As wide planks need much larger stock they had to make do with the narrower planks cut from local trees. This was to have a significant affect on the whole way the Irish boats were to evolve.

*"The Irish builders developed the type in a way different from that of the Shetlanders and built the boats up a couple of strakes on either side. The Skerries yawl has more and narrower planks and considerably less sheer than the fourern. Her keel is longer in relation to overall length"1*

Firstly, the fishermen of the north coast wanted good sailing boats so this may have determined the way that the stem and stern evolved. A straight stem meant less reserve buoyancy in the bow and the boat sliced more smoothly into the waves rather than rise up or be lifted on a rising wave. As Bertie McKay, a fisherman of Portbraddan, Co Antrim so eloquently put it:

1 ibid. Shipping Wonders of the World

**Launching a Drontheim**
UF&TM L1752/7

*"They didn't bang, bang, into the waves, but slid over them... like going into a basin of cream !*

The Caledonian Canal, which had opened in 1822, allowed for easier commercial traffic and influence between Norway, Scotland's north east coast and Ireland. Much of this trade was timber and ice. More 'Dronthons' or Norway yawls came as part of this cargo, on the decks of sailing ships and later steamers coming from the Norwegian ports.

*"As late as August 1834 the Londonderry Shipping Register and General Price Current recorded that the 'Nogaden' from Kristiansund arrived with a cargo of deals, spars, forty three barrels of tar, four boats, and thirty buckets consigned to Samuel Stewart of Ramelton, Co. Donegal"* [1]

Ice was an important cargo because there was a great demand for it from the salmon fisheries of the Foyle and Bann. Each small town had its own primitive cold storage place often cut into a hill or underground to keep the temperature as low as possible. The slope to the harbour in Moville is called the 'ice-house brae' to this day from the great cave almost beneath it where ice was stored.

The men who sailed these timber and ice boats to the Foyle often built small boats at home in Norway in the wintertime and then shipped them, first to the east coast of Scotland and then to Ireland. A generation ago it was remembered in Greencastle that these big cargo ships were often moored for the winter in that part of the Foyle known as 'the South Channel' in the care of members of two local families, the Beatties and Kanes.

## THE FAERING AND THE OSELVER

To identify the Norwegian boats and the characteristics which they brought to the drontheim, we can look at the Norse vernacular boats of today which have remained virtually unchanged over many centuries, so perfectly were they suited to the needs of those who used them.

[1] Ulster Folklife Vol. 28 1982 Michael McCaughan

The boats which came to Ireland probably came from two main regions in Norway. The first and most obvious is the Trondelag region of the north west coast with its great fjord, the Trondheimfjord, and at its mouth the city of Trondheim which gives our Irish boat its unusual name and from which its ancestors were shipped.

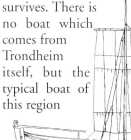

Afjord Faering

This name connection, in fact provides the strongest evidence for its place of origin, at least for those boats which came to Inishowen and the north coast where the name survives. There is no boat which comes from Trondheim itself, but the typical boat of this region

**Drontheim with 'Pleasure Rig'** i.e. Larger mainsail with boom. Whitecastle, Co. Donegal. 1930s
U.F.T.M. L1752/7

Gokstad Ship

which most closely resembles the drontheim gets its name from a nearby village called Afjord and is called the *Afjord Faering.*

The smaller boats of Norway are called faerings, literally 'four-oared boats' These small fjord boats were built for transport and inshore fishing. As the drontheim has varied from region to region across the north coast of Ireland so the faering has offered the same diversity for the Norse regional craftsmen for centuries. In form and structure it has remained, amazingly, almost unchanged since Viking times..

The faering is extremely light and flexible, 18 to 22ft. long , built with a pine keel and five very wide spruce planks per side, and a straight stem and stern. Thwarts are incorporated in substantial transeverse frames. There is a short midships gunwale, strange oar pins called *keips,* three-sided oars, a 'steer-stick' rudder, and

Faering 'Keip"'

a square-sail…very different to the drontheim one might say. Not so. The faering resembles the drontheim much more than would appear at first glance. The straight bow and stern has the same tight curve at the 'turn', and the general size is similar. Both are double-ended, lightly built, but without the former's extreme flexibility. The

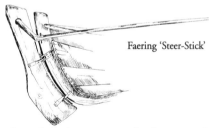

Faering 'Steer-Stick'

drontheim's method of construction, from its scarfed keel, planks, and timbers, to its rudder fittings is entirely Scandanavian. The sandstroke, as we shall see, also provides an interesting common feature. If one carries the faering up

four or five more planks to its high stem and stern, as the Irish boatbuilders must have done, one sees a drontheim emerge!

The drontheim is obviously a much less flexible and 'stiffer' boat due to its extra frames, wearing, and gunwale, but when one looks at an Afjord faering one's eye finds a shape that remembers the lines and shape of a drontheim… a very unscientific method of comparison, but in the absence of hard scientific evidence it is all we can rely on. We can see the 'family connection' between the two boats. The memory if not all the substance of the little fjord boat remains in the drontheim.

Another boat, similar to the faering which may have had an influence on the drontheim's evolution came from the town of Os near Bergen on the same west coast. It is called the *Oselver*, and large numbers of these boats reached the Shetlands in the 18th. and 19th. centuries. We can presume that it may also have reached Ireland in similar fashion.

The oselver had only three very wide planks each side, but a curved stem and stern like the

Killough Yawl

boat in the old Portstewart painting and like those described earlier by

Groomsport Yawl

Sammy Wilkinson as having come to the north coast. It also, similar to the drontheim, carried a sprit-sail and jib.

While the general shape again survived although enlarged and otherwise modified much of its character also survived in the early Groomsport and Killough yawls of Co. Down, other descendants of the

Oselver

Norse imports similar to the drontheim but which carried one or two lug-sails.

And what of the sandstroke? Here is an interesting and real connection. The Norse boats did not have a sandstroke as we know it in Ireland but their first board to the keel was a strange twisted garboard which resembles the sandstroke on a much larger scale. Its existence was recorded a generation ago by the great folklorist Estyn Evans when collecting fishing lore in Co. Down;

**Co. Down Yawl c. 1910**
Note false keel

FISHERMAN'S COTTAGE IN THE KINGDOM OF MOURNE.    WAG 1106

*"It seems the yawls were imported direct from Norway in an unfinished state, carrying only the bottom strake. This garboard strake was a 9in. by 1½in. plank hollowed by adze to a uniform thickness of ³⁄₄in. It was this hollow strake that was the secret of the yawl's seaworthy qualitie ,enabling it to sail close to the wind and keep a steady course. Fitted with a false keel of Mourne holly it took on a local colour and character."*[1]

[1]"Mourne Country" E. Estyn Evans. Dundalgan Press.Dundalk 1967

This board, with a cross-section curving like a bird's wing, bevelled and only nailed to the keel, winds from the vertical at stem and stern to the near horizontal amidships. It arches outward from the keel giving minimum forward resistance below the water-line. It can be seen on the *faering* and *oselver* today, and in both Norway and

America where they still use this technique of hollowing out the garboard strake. It is their most critical board. Whole tree-trunks were once cut specifically for this one board, so important was it. In both Shetland and Norway the keel itself was also sometimes carved and shaped almost like a sandstroke. A hollowed-out centre flared almost to the horizontal at its mid-point and then curved to the vertical again at the bow.

The Irish builders, working in an environment where wide stock was unavailable must have developed the

Carved and hollowed
keel section

sandstroke to achieve the same result for their boat. Combined with the first wide garboard it mimics the Norse 'bird-wing' board. The Irish use two boards for the single Norse hollow garboard to achieve the same effect…an ingenious adaptation to suit their own local needs.

At the turn of the century in Norway to make this complex board a little easier, builders first made a tiny and similar twisted board then fitted a normal wide strake to this in a similar fashion to the Irish builders.

So we have two similar Norse boats of the type which most likely came

**Drontheim Cut in Half**
In use as roof of a sheep shelter, Arranmore Is. 1995

Afjord
Faering

to Ireland generations ago…the *faering* and *oselver*. At the end of the day neither can be definitively identified as the ancestor of our Irish drontheim. It is probably an amalgam of many, a mixture of Norse, Irish, and who knows what influences stretching over centuries. But the drontheim is still at heart a Viking boat, truly part of that same ancient boat-building tradition.

# THE BOAT AND ITS CONSTRUCTION

*"They were a good strong boat. There were hardly ever any accidents in them. She was quite dry and could clean herself in a rough sea".*

(Dan Lafferty)

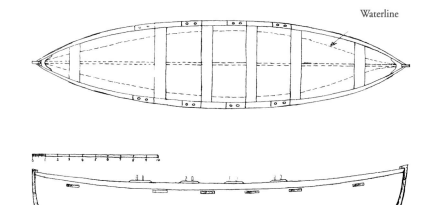

Waterline

The great longships of the Vikings are considered the finest craft constructed by the clinker technique. It enabled these early builders to construct a wonderfully light, flexible, yet extremely strong hull. Building the shell first, with relatively thin overlapping, riveted planks (or strakes) and subsequently adding light frames or ribs (timbers) inside, resulted in a hull which was light yet strong. The most characteristic external feature of a clinker-built boat is this overlap of the planking, which gives it a 'step' form. This hull could flex in a seaway, making a better sea-boat size for size, than the

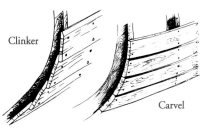

Clinker

Carvel

heavier plank or frame carvel vessels built in Southern Europe. Strength was added to this fragile hull with curved-grain timbers added later, long stringers (or 'wearings') running almost the length of the hull beneath the beams (or thwarts), and finally oak 'side' and 'hanging knees' on the beams, which made a tight yet flexible hull. The carvel boat had heavy flush-laid planks fastened to a pre-erected framework. Its inherent strength made it more suitable for larger and, later, engined boats. Traditionally the clinker hull was shaped without drawings. Measurements and methods were passed from generation to

generation, thus explaining to some extent the conservatism in building techniques and hull form through the centuries. Seemingly frail craft carried Vikings to Greenland and America and its tiny Irish cousin was recorded up to 30 miles north of the Irish coast.

Rather than relying on weight the drontheim took its strength from its clinker method of construction and the precision craftsmanship of its builders. The lines of a sailing drontheim are those of a fast and easily driven craft, her sails driving her with and over the waves and swells rather than into and against

20 ft. Drontheim
Inch Island, Co. Donegal
(Now in Greencastle Maritme Museum)

It was ideally suited to the seas of the north Irish coast, with its great Atlantic swells. It was robust, flexible, easily manoeuverable under sail, able to be rowed over great distances, yet light enough to be hauled ashore by four men on remote beaches or isolated and rocky coves. It was also ideally suited to the salmon, long line fishing and even trawling of the day.

SIZE

Drontheims varied in size from place to place, depending on the needs of the fishermen of that particular area. The smallest seems to have been about 20 ft and was used for example, in the calmer, sheltered waters around Inch island, Co. Donegal. A special 22ft. boat used only for sailing races was built for the fishing communities of West Donegal, Aranmore, Gola, and the Rosses and was sailed with intense competition there. But the 22ft. was most common along the north-east coast, from Portrush as far as Rathlin Island. The 26 ft. boat was the most favoured along the west coast of Donegal and round to the Foyle and would usually be rowed

them unlike the modern-engined boat which batters its way, driven by a different tradition and a more urgent commerce.

There is usually a close logical connection between the form of a boat, its function and the waters in which it is used. These factors are also influenced by economic resources, the strength of tradition and available technology. All these factors came together to produce the drontheim and it changed little from the first photos of the 1870s to the 1950s. It was better suited to local conditions than the heavier carvel-built boats it replaced. These latter are still common in Mayo and Galway where the clinker technique never became popular.

*"Along the Donegal coast, Greencastle yawls, clinker-built, sharp at both ends, light, fast and weatherly, usually painted white or red-lead, and costing about £11 fully found, are rapidly taking the place of the old boats. When loaded with nets or fish they float lighter than the wall-sided boat; and from their sharp-pointed ends, will make better weather when running or when head to sea".* [1]

---

[1] Green W.S "Report of the Inspectors of Irish Fisheries for 1891.

and hauled by four men. They were light enough to be run up on a beach by these same four men and this simple necessity alone often determined the length and weight of the boats. It is related that a boat in Glengad was virtually abandoned by its owner because it was simply too heavy for her normal crew to handle!

West of the Foyle at Glengad, Malin Head and West Donegal a much larger and heavier drontheim was built, up to 28 feet long.

*"There's different water away down there and they had to be cleverer boats".*
(John Jack McLaughlin)

Different conditions and traditions determined the size and style of these larger boats too, and there were local differences.

*"The Greencastle boats were mostly in the shelter. The people from Glengad went further round to the west. I heard their boats called 'Westerd Drontheims'. The Greencastle men would have gone 20 miles from Inishowen Head, to the 'Wee Hill' for long lines".*
(Dan Lafferty)

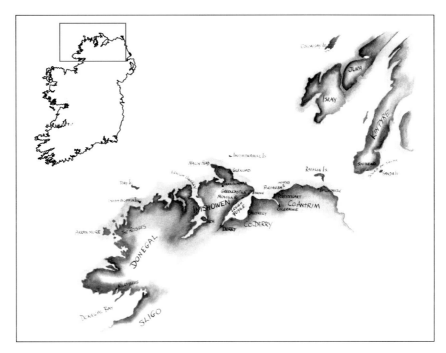

Many fishermen were also small farmers and in addition to fishing, their boats were used for the transport of livestock and other cargo or for the cutting, collection, and transport of great loads of seaweed as manure for the potato crop. It was cut with a scythe blade on a long pole by one man. Another pulled it in with a blunt reaping hook. In the 1930s it could be sold for 16s (80p) a load or even as low as 12s (60p)! Boats were rowed from Greencastle and Strove as far east as the Skerries, off Portrush to cut seaweed. It was considered better quality there! Iron rings in the rocks for tying the boats can be seen there to this day. At one time Inishtrahull Island had 11 families living there and going to the fair in Carndonagh they took in dried fish, pigs, sheep, even horses, in drontheims and took a load of turf back with them!

**Seaweed being cut from a Drontheim**
c.1930, Strove, Co. Donegal
(Note the long handled scythe)

*"The Greencastle yawls on the Inishowen coast and on Tory Island, and other fishing stations in the county Donegal, are worked by men who, as a rule, have small holdings of land, and the receipts from fishing form a most important part of their total receipts".* [1]

## BUILDING

Because of the ready availability of timber from Derry, drontheims could be built for an affordable price. At the beginning of the century drontheims costs about 10s (50p) per foot. By the 1920s this had risen to approximately £1 per foot and the last drontheim built by McDonalds in 1953 cost about £6 per foot. Michael McCaughan states that "about 1890 the Congested Districts Board had large numbers built for poor fishermen in counties Mayo and Galway. The greatest proportion were built for fishermen in County Donegal." [2]

The price for a Moville drontheim in the 1940s was £2 per foot. When timber was scarce (as during World War 11), supplies were obtained locally, unfortunately denuding many areas of trees. Timber was also cut across the Foyle near Ballykelly in what was called 'The Caman Wood'. Many a spar was also cut by night on estates of those who had little time for fishermens' needs. One tree near Clar was related to have been "growing at midnight on Sunday but by Monday morning was dredging mussels". No time for seasoning timber then!

Ironically, Moville and Portrush also exported yawls back to Scotland: notably to the islands of Islay and Colonsay, where they were known as 'Greencastle skiffs' sometimes contracted to 'Greenies', or among gaelic speakers as *'sgoth Eireannach',* (Irish Skiff).

*"They were normally delivered by steamer and at Southend in Kintyre, for example, the Derry-Clyde steamer would heave-to in the sound of Sanda, hoist the new skiff over the side from where it would be managed ashore by a crew from the village".* [1]

Many others, of course, were simply sailed or even rowed across by their new owners.

---

[1] 23rd. Annual Report of the Congested Districts Board for Ireland. 1911.
[2] Michael McCaughan. "Ulster Folk-Life." Vol. 8. 1982.

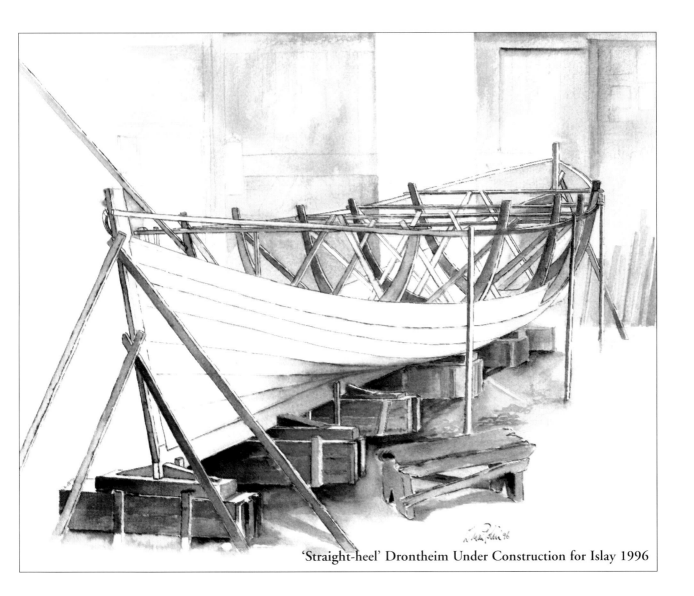

'Straight-heel' Drontheim Under Construction for Islay 1996

# WHAT MAKES THE DRONTHEIM UNIQUE?

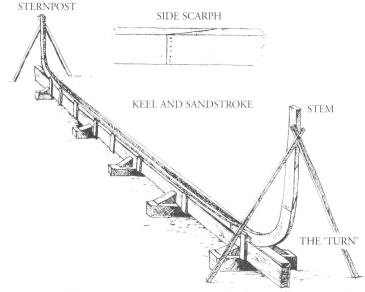

STERNPOST

SIDE SCARPH

KEEL AND SANDSTROKE

STEM

THE 'TURN'

At first glance a drontheim seems to be built in much the same way as contemporary wooden boats, but it has some unique features which are its distinguishing marks and which evolved over a very long period. These can be identified if we look at how one is built and we can see it for the unique craft it is.

Few are alive today who built drontheims in the past but Brian MacDonald of Moville saw them being made and in this section describes many of the traditional methods used.

## THE KEEL

Building began with the keel which was constructed in five main sections. Beginning here the overriding consideration was to keep the boat as light yet as strong as possible - a delicate balance which was superbly realised. The sections were delicately scarphed i.e. joined

sideways unlike the modern horizontal scarphs which are used in heavier keels. Keel sections of the Gokstad ship are side-scarphed in exactly the same way and this style of scarph also seemed to add extra flexibility to the keel, a quality with which the Viking builders were obsessed. Not only was the keel light and narrow, it actually thinned

further to the fine edge of stem and stern. Brian McDonald relates :

*"Keels were always 1¹/₂" (thick). That's all they ever were. The only thing which came down in size was the stem and stern-post from the turn. The turn was actually swelled. The stern was a bit narrower than what the keel was, usually an inch in the difference".*

The keel was also deeper at its mid-point, a feature which had a simple and very practical reason.

KEEL SECTIONS

- eminently practical when boats had to be manoeuvred on narrow beaches and rough coastal paths. The keel of the Gokstad ship also forms an arch from fore to aft:

**New Keel with Sandstroke Fitted Moville 1996**
for Gerard Diver's 24ft. drontheim

Before the keel ever reached the stocks however, the drontheim's most remarkable and age-old feature was first added to it. This was the 'sandstroke', a Norwegian word for the two long, narrow, and tapered boards nailed to both top sides of the keel and which became the first of the 9 boards usually forming the outer hull.

The sandstroke is rarely fitted today, but one of its functions enabled the keel to be easily removed and replaced when necessary.

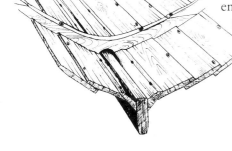

Modern wood boats are built with what is called a 'hog' to which the first boards (garboards), are nailed and also jointed (rebated) into the keel. The interior frames or 'timbers' are then bolted to the keel. These were not bolted in the drontheim.

[1] The Viking Ships. A.W. Brogger and Haakon Shetelig. Hurst and Co. Ltd., London 1971.

In the Viking era there was no connection between the keel and the timbers whatever. They seemed to have found it more practical to let keel and timbers function independently, another aspect of their addiction to flexibility.

Crossing the Atlantic in 1893 in a replica of the Gokstad ship, her captain Magnus Andersen commented :

*"The keel could yield to the movements of the ship, and in a heavy sea would rise and fall as much as $1/4$ of an inch. In a similar sea the gunwale would twist up to 6 inches out of line! All this elasticity, combined with the fine lines, naturally made for speed." [1]*

Once the nails holding the sandstroke to the keel are removed the keel can be easily replaced.

*"In modern ones you have to loose the whole bottom. You have to take off the two garboards and loose the frames too because they are all bolted."*

Looking deceptively simple, the making of a sandstroke took great skill.

*"You make the sandstroke first, before you lay the keel on the stocks. It was actually nailed to the keel before it goes down on the stocks, It was made up on the bench, planed and nailed up and all, up on the bench. The keel was laid then, just with both fore foots on it, and the sandstroke. The sandstroke would stop just before the turn. The keel would be lined up and then the stem and stern posts would be put on it, stayed up, and plumbed up."*

It seems probable that the ancient sandstroke was originally carved directly from the keel itself.

## PLANKING

A clinker boat is built from the outside inwards. The shell of overlapping deal planks is formed first, the rigid framework added afterwards. With the

drontheim this meant that the lower four or five boards are put on first and the oak frames later. These first boards are again part of the unique design of the drontheim. We can see that where they meet the stem or stern post they are quite wide and curve well up the stern and stem. Those following are much narrower. Why is this? The drontheim was primarily an open sailing boat. She had to be dry and easily driven in rough seas. Her hull narrowed significantly at the bow, her profile cutting the water as efficiently and easily as possible. Putting in the first four or five boards high and wide made this narrow bow possible.

[1] ibid. "The Viking Ships"

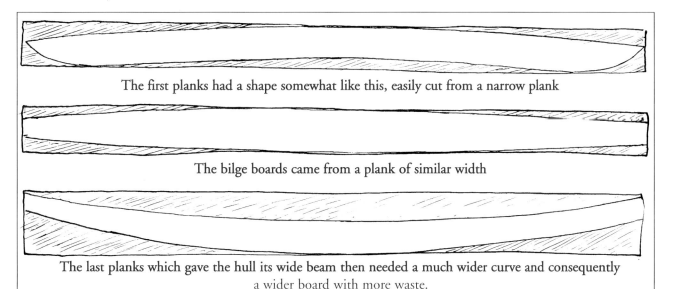

The first planks had a shape somewhat like this, easily cut from a narrow plank

The bilge boards came from a plank of similar width

The last planks which gave the hull its wide beam then needed a much wider curve and consequently a wider board with more waste.

*"She'll throw the water off rather than back into the boat again. If they weren't done that way they would be a lot fuller. You could never keep them in as fine."*

This 'fine' bow meant that the drontheim had a sharp, narrow bow and stern and could "*clean herself in a big sea*" as the local expression goes. This worked also for high following seas as for driving into waves;

*"It's a finer boat, both for'ard and aft for sailing and rowing. They weren't built for an engine. For sailing purposes they were built fine, very fine."*

The 'finer' bow or stern could be planked from narrow flitches of timber, (a flitch is a plank cut from the full width available from the tree), an important advantage when timber was scarce or trees were of small circumference. A 'fuller' bow or stern needed a wider plank A finer more efficient bow meant less wood as well.

*"The higher up you can get the first three or four, and on the bigger ones five (boards), the higher up you get them you have a cleaner boat, for a start off. Also, the planking on the top sides is easier cut out. The thing was, when the boat builders were cutting trees themselves, there were no great lumps of trees, so the higher up they got these here (the first boards), the more they were going to get out of the trees they were cutting. The stuff was scarce then!"*

Brian McDonald

Whether the availability of timber or the demands of finer sailing determined the design of the drontheim, we do not know.

The patterns or 'moulds' for the outer shell of the boat were added next. These are wooden patterns assembled from rough pieces cut to the shape of the timbers and set up temporarily to the keel. Over these the planking is laid. At a later stage these moulds are removed and the timbers inserted. Before the days of paper plans all the measurements were taken from a beautiful half-model, built to scale. This was used for generations and was designed more by the boatbuilder's accurate eye than by drawn plans.

**Fitting the 'Moulds'**, McDonalds, Moville

Half Model

But before that there was a time when all boats were designed by experience, built by hand and eye alone, without drawings or models but from the knowledge and good sense that had passed through generations of intelligent and resourceful people. They understood the demands of the sea and the potential of the wood that they shaped and fitted with such reverence and precision. Something of that same inherited wisdom can be seen in boats by McDonalds today. Like the Norse boats much of the drontheim's final shape was determined by the eye of the builder and the quality and width of the plank stock. The sheer-line was determined by the sheer battens and moulds and was done almost completely by eye, the battens being fixed and re-fixed in the earthen floor until the lines were 'right'. No two boats were ever totally alike.

The divisions in the half model correspond to the main 'moulds' and between them went the graceful timbers (the boat's ribs) after the outer boards had been fitted. The moulds themselves correspond roughly to where the beams or seats were when added later. The planks were of ⁹⁄₁₆ in. deal and were built up in stages from the keel and sandstroke, planks first, then timbers.

A 'Westerd' Drontheim, which belonged to Hugh McCann, Strove, Co. Donegal, 1984.

These planks, usually in two pieces, were joined like the keel by a delicate side-scarph. The outer edge of the scarph always pointed aft so as to shed water as the boat was in motion.

Before each new plank was added, its lower edge (which would overlap the top edge of the previous plank), was painted with a line of Archangel tar on top of which was a line of

woollen yarn. This formed an internal watertight seal between the two planks, a technique unchanged since Viking times :

*"Loose woolly threads were spun into a thick cord. The caulk was dipped in tar and placed in a groove near the lower edge of every strake, so that it was pressed tightly together when the planking was rivetted".[1]*

1. ibid. "The Viking Ships"

The Viking ship also had a delicate beading all along the lower edge of all its planks. On the drontheim this survives only on the gunwale strake, along the edges of the beams, and on the wearing.

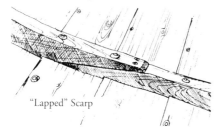

"Lapped" Scarp

Once again, in order to keep the boat as light as possible when it was necessary to join the different sections of the timbers, a 'lapped' scarf was used rather than the more modern side scarph join. This produced an interior of great lightness and flexibility, less rigid than the modern method, possibly more prone to cracking in heavy

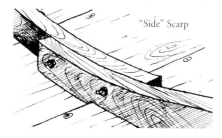

"Side" Scarp

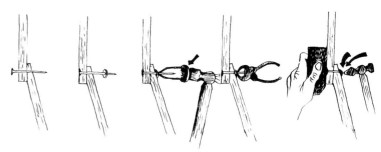

Rooving two Planks

seas but infinitely more pleasing to the eye. Originally all timbers were cut and shaped from a piece of oak that was naturally curved by growth. The older drontheim's unique lap-scarphed timbers seem to echo this earlier practice before timber became scarce and the modern side-scarph became necessary.

The planks were then 'rooved' or riveted to these timbers with copper nails. The Gokstad ship's planking was similarly joined. Round-headed rivets were driven through both planks from the outside. On the inside, the nails were riveted over a little iron plate called a 'clinch-plate'. In the Norse this plate is called a 'ro'. The English 'roove' is an obvious derivation.

In Donegal this is sometimes termed 'Rooved Throughout', meaning that planks are riveted to timbers and planks to each other. There was a drontheim once in Greencastle rooved with halfpennies during World War II when copper rooves were in short supply. It was known thereafter as 'The ould halfpenny boat'.

This desire for lightness also produced another unique drontheim feature - bow planks were nailed directly to the stern and stem rather than jointed (or rebated into them) - producing an extremely fine and delicate finish to the planks at the bow.

*"All the ends of the boards were just scarphed directly on to the stern. They weren't rebated in.*

*There were no rebates because the keels were light and the stem and stern posts were light. They had to be as light as possible, mainly for haulin', maybe one or two crews landing at one time, you'd be depending on them two crews to haul each other's boat."*

Once again we hear of the need for lightness and flexibility reflecting the old Viking obsession. A commentator in Norway writing in 1881 about the Gokstad ship could be describing the drontheim also:

*"The boat must have possessed a pliancy and mobility in a heavy sea which we should look upon as ominous in a modern sea-going craft. Her real safety consisted in a tough and elastic outer skin, which would be the more invulnerable from not being made unduly rigid at any point. Thus her apparent weakness was her strength".[1]*

Flooring was sparse. Three or more narrow, flat laths were laid on each side of a centre board running along the keel, all hooked and pegged into place. There was a small platform

**Bow of Old Drontheim**, Malin Head 1985

for the man at the tiller, another at the bow.

## TOOLS

Tools varied little over the centuries as well and in the old boat yards could be found the essential tools of the shipwright; the adze, the auger, the clamp, the spoke-shave and the jack-plane. Remarkably similar tools were found in the Viking ship graves, again showing the continuity of tradition.

Drontheims were rarely built strictly to the usual 26ft length or 6ft 8in. beam. Buyers inevitably wanted two or three inches more or less here and there. To accommodate this, the fore and aft moulds could be 'stretched' to make the boat a few inches longer.

That changed the position of the beams slightly but what difference could a couple of inches make?

*"Well, the neighbours always wanted one a wee bit bigger than the other one. That went on down*

1. ibid "The Viking Ships"

**Michael Doherty's Dromtheim with Fishing Rig**
Port Ronan, Malin, Co. Donegal 1985
(Now in Maritime Museum, Greencastle.)

*through the years. Sometimes they went about with a stick, one measuring the other one, to see who had the bigger boat!"*

For example, the record of two drontheims sold in Malin Head in the same year 1914.

*1. P.A. Doherty, Malin Head. 26 x 6.6 x 2.7. Rooved throughout. £13:10:0.*

*2. Thos. Doherty (Robert), Malin Head. 26 x 6.8 x 2.9. Copper throughout £14:13:0!*

Two inches on beam and depth cost an extra £1:3 shillings!

The extraordinary variations in length and beam which can be seen in the McDonald sales records *(see Appendix II)* suggest also that fishermen developed their own preferences in size through experience over generations in boat

handling and carrying capability and the differences were no mere social one-upmanship. Such was the reputation of good builders like the Beatties or McDonalds that buyers often came from great distances to buy boats from them and then sailed or rowed them home rather than rely on the work of some local whose work did not have the tradition or reputation of the others.

But it was no easy life. All-weather winter long-line fishing from an open boat and pulling a great oar for hours was not for the faint-hearted. By the 1950s times had changed and the sailing drontheim almost disappeared overnight.

The invention of the marine engine and its local availability, improved nets and gear, better harbour facilities and fiercer competition brought a different style of boat with greater comfort and speed, safety and different commercial incentives. The drontheim was quickly replaced by the diesel-engined half-decker and there was little nostalgia for the old hardships of sail and oar. But power robbed us of the sight of this sweet-

**Beattie Built Drontheim Motor Boat, Moville**
c.1980s

lined and elegant craft, a loss to the armchair lovers of sail but not to the generations of men who slaved at the long oars or shivered in freezing temperatures with fingers crooked by holding cold and wet lines. There was little regret at their passing.

However, such was the respect of the sailing drontheim that the new engined boats were often little changed from the original design apart from the stern tube and engine. Sails and oars were carried for many years by the older men who never really had faith in the engines. Some drontheims also had their stern posts modified to take a propeller and an in-board engine and they gave many more years of service. Often, however, they were so heavily modified that only the long clean lines of the old sailing boat can be seen below half-decks, higher sheers, wheel houses and engines. A few remain to this day: a reminder to only a few of a different world.

# THE BUILDERS

Until the middle of this century the builders of a Norwegian faering or an Irish drontheim would have worked in a very conservative and isolated tradition. Boat design, once perfected, was religiously respected and the tradition guarded. There was little outside influence and the old boat-builders rarely travelled from the areas in which they lived and worked. Traditional methods were passed from father to son. For example, laying the keel was often a secret one boat-builder would not let another one see, and especially the fitting of a sandstroke. This was often made and fitted at night and the first thing an outsider saw next day was keel, sandstroke, and the first two boards, all set up and ready.

The local area supplied most of the boat-builder's needs apart from the imported spruce or 'deal'. He selected and cut his own timber. The local blacksmith forged the iron. The fishermen themselves cut

Brian McDonald, Moville and the Islay "Irish Skiff" 1996 (Derry Journal 5/7/A201

and sewed the cotton sails. The McDonalds, Beatties, and the Portrush builders used local timber when it was available, but all cut oak, larch and some spruce in the Caman Wood near Ballykelly in Co. Derry till the 1950s. Oak and larch were also cut at Loughguile in Co. Antrim by the Portrush builders. The trees were felled carefully so as to preserve as many of the curved branches as possible which would provide the 'swept-grain' (naturally curved) timbers, breast-hooks, knees and crooks. Careful husbandry preserved this valuable local resource for a long time. With the war and the end of wood imports most of the local wood was devastated, never to recover. Today the curved-grain oak-wood, once so valuable, is largely discarded by sawmills in favour of the straight grain for floor or furniture.

Two Drontheims Being Built in McDonalds' Shed, Moville 1999

Two groups of builders made most of the north coast yawls, at Portrush, Co. Antrim, and Moville Co. Donegal. The McCann brothers of Moneygold in Sligo also built yawls. Both still build today.

McDonalds of Moville are one of the oldest boat-building families in these islands. Coming originally from Scotland in 1750 they built first at Greencastle, and 50 years later settled in Moville, just three miles away. There are they to this day. Their fine craftsmanship can be seen in the great variety of clinker-built boats all round the north coast and elsewhere. Two of their fine sailing drontheims can be seen today, the 26ft. one built for Islay in 1996, and a restored 24ft. one now sailing at Moville.

It is quite possible that the McDonalds, working in Greencastle, originally copied and then modified

**Restored 24¹⁄₂ft Gola Island 'Skiff'**
Lough Foyle Aug. 1997

the Norwegian boats which had been dropped here from the big trading schooners from Trondheim. Firstly called 'Drontheims' they were later registered as 'Greencastle yawls'. As they were sold on to other areas different local names evolved as we shall see; e.g. 'Skiff', 'Skerries Yawl', 'Norway yawl', 'Irish skiff', 'Shallop' etc.

Another family working in Moville was the Beatties, two brothers Willie and Archie, whose last boat was built about 1945 or 1946. While there was rivalry, naturally, between them and McDonalds, it was friendly and there was enough work for both. Over the years great numbers of yawls were built in Moville. Tradition has it that the Beatties built a lighter and 'finer'

boat, McDonalds, a stronger and slightly heavier working boat.

Lighter scantlings, fineness and attention to details such as the delicate curved beading on the end of a wearing, the graceful long curve of a knee, the short curved timber beneath a beam…all are distinctly Beattie. Their working boat was built with the same grace as their sailing punts, made light to sail and row fast. A similar fragile grace can be seen in Gerard Diver's Gola yawl which was built by a builder in Bunbeg called Gallagher of whom little is known.

McDonalds were no lesser craftsmen, the Beatties simply added a lighter and more decorative extra 'something'.

*"Of all the drontheim builders the Beatties were the tidiest of the lot. The finish was first class. Old Willie was a perfectionist. When you'd look along that line between bow and stern that sweet curve was lovely"*

(Arthur Mc Elnay)

But there was a danger in having too fine a bow. As narrated by

**Modified Beattie boat
Ballintoy Horbour 1997**

Sammy Gault, a man named Conway in Dunseverick moulded a boat off a Beattie one but he made it too fine. An old Rathlin man called John Hegarty took a look over it.

*"What do you think of her John?"
"Great work" he said, "I never seen anything better." but then added, "If you were runnin' before a brave breeze and stemmin' (going against) the tide, I'm afraid you'd loss her. The too fine bow would put the head down...."*

This happened also if they were converted to take engines. A Beattie boat generally went down at the stern while the McDonald boat, fuller at bilge and beam took the engine better.

Of course no two drontheims were ever completely alike. The eye of the builder and the character of each plank often dictated the final shape of the boat as can be seen in the endless variations among McDonalds' records. The fishermen themselves all along the north coast still dispute the qualities of the different builders and bought equally from both families. The fact that the Beatties were Presbyterian and the McDonalds Catholic no doubt added to the debate, and a little religion, as always in Ireland, might enter to bias the placing of an order!

The Beatties never passed on their skills and both were dead by the mid 1950s. They were, perhaps, typical of that age when the skills of the boatbuilder or blacksmith brought them great status within their communities and their secrets would only be passed on to family. When there was none, or even if there was, they kept their skills and they died with them. A story is told that the last old Beattie had all his plans and moulds for boats burned shortly before his death. Old Jimmy Kelly of Portrush, however, seems to have been the exception and he passed on many of his skills before he died. Of the Beattie boats only their sailing punts survive. A beautifully restored Beattie drontheim with an engine fitted, can be seen in Ballintoy harbour, Co. Antrim, today.

In Portrush the great Victorian boatbuilder was James Hopkins. Boat-building had begun there in

**The McCanns of Moneygold, Sligo, in a yawl that they built** c. 1900.
Johnny 'Rua' *(seated)*, sons - Thomas and John - and a neighbour James Gillen

New Dronthon Deals and Train Oil.

CUNNINGHAM GREG is just landing out of the Brig Success, from Dronthon, a Cargo of Deals of the very first quality; also a few barrels of Train Oil, which he will dispose of on reasonable terms.

Belfast, 24th June, 1789.

To be let and entered upon from the first day of No-

**From the Belfast Telegraph 1789**

the last century when the big timber boats brought wood from Boston and Philadelphia, off-loading cargo here to reduce their draught to get up the river Bann to Coleraine. Pine had been the timber imported until about 1800 when it changed to spruce. Norwegian spruce planks were called 'deals', so giving the name to the white or red 'deal' so common today. In their heyday the Portrush builders sent great numbers of yawls to Scotland as well as all round the north coast. Running on the flood tide from the

Bull Point on Rathlin a boat could make Islay in 3 ½ hours!

James Kelly was Hopkin's apprentice and built in Portrush till his death in the early 1950s. He was a great designer/craftsman, not just of drontheims, but of all kinds of wooden boats. His shed was at the edge of the White Rocks sands there, so close to the sea that it sometimes came up and almost in to where he worked. All trace of that boatyard is long gone.

*"Kelly's boat was heavier built for man-hauling on the beaches. That's*

*why the Inishowen boats scored here. They were as strong, but lighter put together, as the man says, 'a tighter boat'."*
(Sammy Gault, Dunseverick)

Two Kelly boats only remain today. One is the 26ft. 'Catherine' built for Donald MacFarlane of Islay, now in Portrush Boat Museum. The second is a 22ft. built for Islay but sold to the Wilkinsons of Ballintoy Co. Antrim. When the Islaymen arrived over to collect it, but without sufficient money, Kelly wouldn't give it to them! They rowed back empty-handed. It too, alas, now also lies derelict. These two boats provide a unique insight into the superb craftsmanship of Kelly as we shall see when we look at the story of the yawls on Islay.

Tom and John McCann of Moneygold, Co. Sligo and their father before them built yawls for Donegal Bay, from 26ft. to 28ft. from local larch and oak. Yawls died out here in the 1940s but they built a fine larch 26ft in 1998, with a sandstroke!

# LIFE ON THE DRONTHEIMS

*"The fishermen that's going now wouldn't stick it long."*
(Barney McKenny, Glengad)

The world of the Donegal drontheim fisherman a generation or two ago, as the old men tell us, was vastly different from that of today. Before the marine engine and modern technology, the fishing way of life and conditions would have changed little for many generations. It was tough, dangerous and uncertain work. Hardship was common. Equipment was often inadequate, improvisation the norm rather than the exception. Prices for the catch rarely matched the labour involved, but it was all there was. The following section draws heavily on the reminiscences of a generation of Donegal fishermen whose world has passed almost without record.

## ROWING

*"The first oar I rowed in a drontheim boat was an eighteen foot oar. Ould Nealie Walker used to say to me "Them boys that are fishing now wouldn't be much good on an 18 foot oar!".*
(Henry Canning)

As with the size of the drontheim, the oar size varied from place to place. The most common 26ft. boat

**Rowing to Innishtrahull Island, Co. Donegal**
Note heavy 'box' oars 'double banked'
Courtesy H. Tinney, Culdaff

took an 18ft. oar. These were rounded along their full length and where they rested on the gunwale (or 'rowth' as the small hardwood platform for the oar was locally called) they were often bound with rope to save the wood being worn. Tying on this rope was a skill in itself and was called 'Roping an Oar'. The oar was then held between two wooden pins, usually of hardwood but often hazel or ash. Oars were generally of white deal or pine, and because of the use of pins could be 'feathered' if necessary. 'Feathering' was a way of flattening the oar horizontally to the surface of the water with a twist of the wrist as the oar was lifted from the water and brought forward after each stroke. It was a way of reducing the oar's wind resistance in a head wind thereby increasing speed, as Bob Kavanagh put it :

*"It was hard to row into a breeze of wind".*

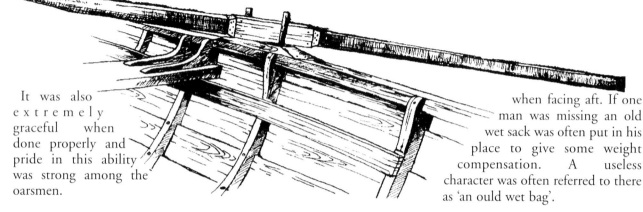

It was also extremely graceful when done properly and pride in this ability was strong among the oarsmen.

The larger 28 foot 'westerd' drontheims, often crewed by up to seven men had 18 ft.oars and even a 21 ft. oar which was called 'a great oar' or a sweep.

*"They were a great big boat. You could play football on them!"*
(John Jack McLaughlin)

These oars differed substantially from the 16ft. ones in that they were what was called 'boxed' oars, i.e. the section of the oar coming between the pins (or 'towpins' as they were called in Glengad), was left square. These oars could not be rotated and so could not be feathered. Protective wood pieces called 'wearing boards'

or 'cleats' were nailed to the sides of this boxed section and took the main wear and tear on the oar. They could be replaced when necessary.

In Glengad these great oars were so heavy they were often 'double banked' i.e. rowed by two men. This was the arrangement when seven men would go out for long-line fishing in the winter. Two men would be on the bow and main oars, one each on the main aft and aft oars and the last man was on the tiller. The most important oar was the main oar. The others took their stroke from the aft oar or 'stroke' oar. It was always rowed on the port side or the oarsman's right hand side

when facing aft. If one man was missing an old wet sack was often put in his place to give some weight compensation. A useless character was often referred to there as 'an ould wet bag'.

Rowing was hard and cruel work, especially with a contrary tide but the men knew nothing else.

*"People were used to it, that's what I'm saying. If you weren't used to it, and hadn't the practice, even if you were as strong as a horse, you wouldn't stick it! But when you were used to that rowing you could row all day. Oh aye, it was a sore life!"*

(Henry Canning)

And at the end of a long row back from the fishing grounds, boats had to be unloaded of nets and ballast and then pulled up on a beach.

Most boats were kept on beaches or pulled up in 'ports' (small natural harbours). Proper moor-ing piers or harbours were few and anyway it was necessary to have large open areas nearby where nets could be spread to be cleaned and dried after each night's fishing for salmon.

*"They were made light enough for four men to pull up. They were big boats, but once you got them on the sticks, good green sticks, by Lord they could slide along. Everybody had their own sticks. They always cut them for salmon fishing."*

(Henry Canning)

Drontheims were often slid up the beach on the backs of skate if a lot had been caught, not at the price that can be got for them today of course!

*"They fished a lot away over by Portstewart and Portrush and round there at the back of the Head (Shrove Head). They used to shoot (the net) in the river here on an ebb tide and drive on out of the river away out to the nor'ard to board. And if they got a breeze of wind they would sail back, if not, they had to get on four oars and row back, against the tide. It was a hard ould life."*

(Henry Canning)

There were four oar positions on board a working drontheim. First, nearest the stem was the 'bow oar'. Next came the 'main oar' on the opposite side. Then the 'waist' or 'main after oar' and finally the 'stern or 'aft' oar. A fifth man, the skipper usually, would have taken the tiller. Often the boat was steered by oars alone with the aft oarsman taking a bearing from the stern and directly the course. He was then termed rowing 'stroke' i.e. determined the speed and strength of all the oars which were based on his oar.

Three men might also row while the fourth steered and compensated with the tiller for the missing man. The aft oar was considered a beginner's oar. On the big "westerd" drontheims two men would often be double banked on two great oars and one on each of the others, these other oars being smaller. A 'foot board' or 'foot-spur' to give support to the oarsman's feet, was often used and could be adjusted to suit the individual's leg length.

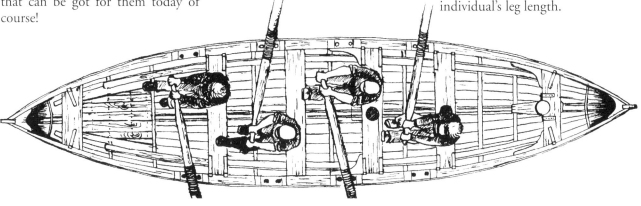

## SAILING

Most drontheims were worked with a single, unstayed mast, setting a loose-footed sprit sail, and a single jib, set flying from the stem-head (without a bow-sprit). This allowed a relatively large area of sail to be set without taking up space in the boat when the rig was taken down for fishing operations or when rowing. This simple rig could be stepped or un-stepped out at sea.

The drontheim had three positions for masts and this allowed for different local rigs. For example, Inisboffin Island drontheims were normally sailed with two masts set in the first and third beams. Generally, however, the single mast was stepped in the second beam from the bow (the 'main' beam).

Masts were stepped in the boat using two distinct arrangements at the thwart or beam with a circular socket arrangement for the heel of

**Drontheim near Burtonport, Co. Donegal**
The normal fishing rig of spritsail and jib has been set to catch the light airs
Courtesy U.F.T.M. L2296/9

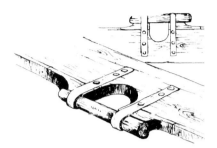

the mast called a 'step' or 'shoe' which was fitted across the timbers below the beam.

The first arrangement at the beam was simply a hole through it to accommodate the mast. Though simple, this rendered stepping the mast at sea much more difficult as the heel of the mast had to be raised up to the level of the beam to allow the entire mast to be dropped through the hole. The second, more efficient arrangement incorporated either a metal 'mast-gate' or a distinctive wooden wedge arrangement fitted on the aft or

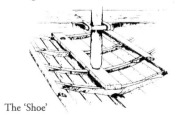

The 'Shoe'

for'ard side of the beam. This allowed the heel of the mast to be placed into the 'shoe' before raising it upright and clamping it in position - a more manageable operation entirely! Mast and sprit-sail were generally lifted as one, the sails always being stored already bent to the mast, with the sprit alongside.

Mast and wrapped sail would sometimes project out over the bow and down under the main beam. If the clasp was on the for'ard side of the beam the mast then came easily and neatly up to it where it would be tightened in with a small hardwood peg or the 'gate' was closed, locked with a securing metal pin and wedges knocked in alongside the mast to tighten it.

'Mast-gate' or clasp

The stepping of the mast is described by the late Dan Lafferty :

*"The sail was called a 'shoulder-of-mutton' sail (this refers to its shape). All the rigging was done in about 3 minutes. The mast was down with the sail wrapped around it and the sprit alongside. One man stood facing the bow, and a man stood behind him and put the top of the mast over his shoulder. Then the man behind stepped forward shouting "forward" and pushing the mast up. The bow man then steadied it down and into position in the shoe They pulled open the sail and handed the 'leads' (sheets), back to the skipper who was going to steer. The man in the front passed the sprit back to the second man who pushed it into the top peak of the sail. He raised it in one go and put the beckit down low enough to catch the other end of the sprit. He pushed the sprit up to make the sail completely tight and then pushed up the beckit. If it slipped on the mast, water was thrown on it to tighten it up. Sometimes there were two guy ropes or strengthening ropes attached to the mast and he tied these down to the beam that the mast was in. They set the jib after that."*

As often as not the mast had no stays, but as the jib halliard was brought back through the mast head-pulley, this was tied down to a beam and served as a mast stay.

This jib halliard (locally called the 'hallya') in some drontheims at Glengad was taken down to a cleat in the gunwale made with a wood pin and an iron receiver, locally referred to as a 'dule' or 'dool'.

The jib-sheet was often put to small 'belaying pins' underneath the

The 'Dule'

gunwale and always with a running end because as Bob Cavanagh said:

"*No man in his right senses would tie a knot in the jib sheet. That's how you were lost.*"

A jib sheet might also be simply put around the 'wearing' (known also as a 'bearer') if belaying pins were absent or broken. The skipper

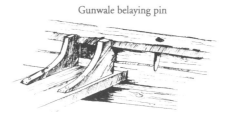

Gunwale belaying pin

then took the main sheet rope round a beam or round stout wood pegs which projected aft from the last beam. With the tiller he now controlled the boat to a great degree.

The jib, however, was the crucial sail. It required careful handling and drove the boat more so than the mainsail.

"*If there was a lot of wind in it you wouldn't chance the wearing, but took it round the beam. The man in the bow had the jib rope and he took a turn round the peg under the gunwale if there was one. If she got a bad 'fla' (gust) of wind he slacked off. If there was a terrible lot of wind and you running before it they put no sprit in at all. They tied the top down and it would flap away. A 'barmoody' they called it! It was simple sailing.*"

(Henry Canning)

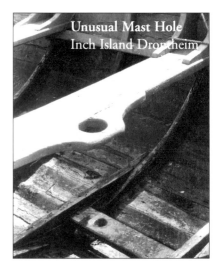

**Unusual Mast Hole**
Inch Island Drontheim

In Glengad taking out the sprit was described as "making a goer of her"! Simple it may have appeared but there was no room on such boats for the foolish or the incompetent. These were the days before life-jackets or distress flares. A sailing drontheim carried only her crew and gear, oars and heavy ballast. There was no room for mistakes or incompetence.

Although the drontheim was an entirely open boat she was very dry in a rough sea. When sailed properly, she could 'clean herself' in a heavy sea.

**Stern Beam Peg to take main sheet**

## BALLAST

A 26 foot drontheim took upwards of a ½ ton of ballast, all of which had to be unloaded after each fishing trip before the boat was hauled out. It was re-loaded for the next trip again. Generally ballast consisted of large stones, sandbags only appearing after the war. But not just any old stones were suitable. They had to be rounded so as to avoid the possibility of a pointed edge breaking through a plank. Their careful placing was crucial to the boat's trim and handling and in sailing, ballast had to be moved as the ship changed tack. In Glengad ballast was often done up in old net because cloth or hessian bags would last little time. They would rot and be cut by the stones.

There were also superstition in the choosing of stones for ballast. Danny O'Sullivan when light-keeper on Inishtrahull relates how ballast stones collected on the beach could not have white stones among them. These were 'fairy stones'. Similarly, 'whin' stones found near the base of a whin (gorse) bush were considered unlucky. Bad luck could not be courted when out at sea in a frail open boat.

Henry Canning has described how ballast was kept out from shore on a rock near the Warren Light close to Greencastle called 'Rabins Rock'. At one time a great many drontheims were pulled up at the beach there, and when going to sea the boats were first launched and rowed over to the rock. Two men got out on the rock and loaded the ballast stones while the others steadied the boat. The same ballast was then similarly unloaded on the way back. Each crew had its own particular stones and some remain there to this day, the boats and men long gone.

## REGATTAS

Sailing was very different for the regattas, held generally at the end of the salmon season. For racing at Glengad two mainsails were used and a long bowsprit or 'jib-stick' carried one or even two jibs. The second main was often borrowed as boats rarely could afford the luxury of two mainsails! With such a rig one can imagine the speed and

Drontheims racing at Glengad, Co. Donegal, c 1950.
U.F.T.M. L1752/5/6

excitement of such heavily canvassed boats on a breezy day.

At Moville, different rules applied. Here a specially made gaff-rigged mainsail and boom was used. Because of the variety in size of the working sails and the advantage larger sail would give, it was decided to standardise the sails. In the 50s, the new sails were ordered and three were made (it would seem for the last three sailing drontheims left) These were enormous sails and took

skilled handling. Taking water was always a risk as they raced in a high wind.

*"It was rarely if ever you needed to bail her, only when you were sailing in races she would take water continuously on her lee side. That's what they put the washboards on for".*

(Dan Lafferty)

'Washboards' were temporary extra planks fitted round the sides when a

boat was specially rigged for racing. These boards prevented a weight of water coming aboard amidships when the boat was well- heeled over under a large press of sail. To reduce drift from such huge sails false keels made from long planks of wood nailed or bolted to the keel were sometimes used but were generally forbidden!

As the sails were all made by different makers naturally some were considered superior to others. A draw had to be held before each race to allocate the sails. These were called the 'The Big Rig', in comparison to smaller sails normally used when fishing. With ever larger sails, more ballast, washboards, and false keels, the elegant sprit-rigged fishing drontheim became an

The 'Big-Rig' and 'Washboards' on a Drontheim at Moville c. 1950s

ungainly monster, increasingly ridiculous, inefficient and ultimately dangerous.

As they disappeared from the fishing grounds in the early fifties the last regattas to feature drontheims were in 1950 and 1951.

But they had been magnificent events when crowds came by steamer from Derry and there is a hint of nostalgia for the lost days of the 'Empire' in the following extract from the Londonderry Standard Aug. 1st. 1931;

## "A MOST USEFUL CLASS OF MEN"

"These races took place on Monday last and went off with great affect. They were a source of innocent amusement to many thousands of spectators, and altogether presented a scene truly enlivening, whether one beheld the happy faces of the spectators who lined the shore of the beautiful bay of Moville or the hundreds of boats which gaily skimmed its magnificent expanse of water. Many of our citizens participated in the enjoyment. They were conveyed thither by the steamer Londonderry, on board of which was the band of the 58th. who performed in the finest style "Rule Brittania" and a variety of other national airs.

In the third race the rowers were female; their costume was sufficiently light for the season, and for the severe exercise they had undertaken. They seemed as expert, and as much at home in propelling their skiffs; as any of their sex in the Society Islands could be....

There are to be more boat races here today, at one o'clock. The organizers have been unwearily exerting themselves for the gratification of the public, and the encouragement of a most useful class of men.

The party in the Londonderry enjoyed themselves well on their return. If there was not wassail, there was wine, wit, and quadrilles!"

Drontheims racing at Moville c. 1930's (Courtesy: W. Bigger, Derry)

# MOVILLE ANNUAL
# REGATTA

WILL BE HELD

## ON MONDAY, 5TH AUGUST, 1935,

Commencing at ELEVEN o'clock a.m.

## PROGRAMME:

### REGATTA RACES.

**1st Race.** Sailing Race for Drontheim Fishing Boats, any rig, not exceeding 26ft. keel. Fins not allowed.

First Prize, £6. 2nd Prize, £4. 3rd Prize, £2. Entrance Fee, 2/6

**2nd Race.** Rowing Race. Four-Oared Punts. For Schoolboys under 16 years.

First Prize, £1. 2nd Prize, 10/. 3rd Prize, 5/. Entrance Free.

**3rd Race.** Rowing Race. Open. 1 Man. For punts not exceeding 16ft. keel.

First Prize, 10/. 2nd Prize, 6/. 3rd Prize, 4/.

**4th Race.** Rowing Race. Open, for Paired-oared Punts not exceeding 16ft. keel.

First Prize, £1. 2nd Prize, 10/. 3rd Prize, 5/. Entrance Fee, 1/.

**5th Race.** Rowing Race. Four-Oared Drontheim Fishing Boats, not less than 25ft. keel, 6ft. 4in. beam, 2ft. 5in. deep.

First Prize, £4. 2nd Prize, £2. 3rd Prize, £1. Entrance Fee, 2/.

**6th Race.** Sailing Race. Open. for Punts not exceeding 16ft. keel; outside keel not to exceed 3 inches; any rig.

First Prize, £3. 2nd Prize, £2. 3rd Prize, £1. Entrance Fee, 2/.

 ## SPORTS

**Aquatic Sports at Old Stone Pier**

commencing at 3 p.m.

| | FIRST PRIZE | 2ND | 3RD |
|---|---|---|---|
| 1. Schoolboys' Swimming Race. | 5s 0d | 2s 6d | 2s |
| 2. Men's Swimming Race. | 7s 6d | 4s 0d | 2s |
| 3. Comical Boat and Land Race. | 10s 0d | 7s 6d | 5s |
| 4. Shovel Race. One man | 5s 0d | 4s 0d | 3s |
| 5. Shovel Race. Two men | 8s 0d | 4s 0d | 2s |
| 6. Ladies' Swimming Race | 7s 6d | 4s 0d | 2s |

**SHORE SPORTS at Bath Green**

commencing at 4 p.m.

| | FIRST PRIZE | 2ND | 3RD |
|---|---|---|---|
| 1. Boys under 16, Flat Race, 100 Yds. | 5s 0d | 3s 0d | 2s |
| 2. Girls under 16, Flat Race, 100 Yds. | 5s 0d | 3s 0d | 2s |
| 3. Relay Race, 4 in each Team, 440 Yds. | £1 | 12s 0d | 8s |
| 4. Human Wheelbarrow Race. | 5s 0d | 4s 0d | 2s |
| 5. Three-Legged Race. | 5s 0d | 4s 0d | 2s |
| 6. Ladies' Flat Race | 5s 0d | 3s 0d | 2s |
| 7. Race for Schoolboys | 4s 0d | 2s 0d | 1s |
| 8. Race for Schoolgirls | 4s 0d | 2s 0d | 1s |

**TUESDAY, 6th AUGUST, A FIVE-A-SIDE FOOTBALL COMPETITION will be held in the Bay Field, commencing at 3 p.m.**

## RULES

1. Starts in Sailing Races to be made under weight. A Preparatory Gun will be fired Five minutes before Start of Sailing Race. Any Boat breaking the Line before the Second Gun will be recalled, and must recross the Line, or be disqualified. Course to be deemed completed when Boat breaks the Line at finish of Race.

2. No Race unless 2 Boats compete. No 2nd Prize unless 3 compete. No Third Prize unless 4 compete.

3. Any Boat deliberately fouling another, or fouling any Mark, will be disqualified.

4. Protests in writing, with £1 Deposit must be lodged with the Committee within One Hour of completion of the Race.

5. The decision of the Committee in all cases is final.

6. The Committee reserve the right of postponing the Regatta should the weather, in their opinion, be unfavourable.

7. All Entries must be made with the Hon. Sec. not later than TEN o'clock on Morning of Regatta.

8. No Entry accepted unless accompanied by Entrance Fee.

## A BAND WILL BE IN ATTENDANCE

COMMITTEE WILL NOT BE RESPONSIBLE FOR ANY ACCIDENT.

The County Donegal Printing Co., Ltd., Letterkenny

## CHARLES SWEENEY, Hon. Sec.

A Glengad Drontheim at Greencastle Regatta 18th August 1951

# FISHING

*"The fishermen at that time (early '20s), would let you out if you carried the water. All the drinking water had to come from St. Columcille's well. The tap water was no good for taking to sea".*

(Dan Lafferty)

Holy Water and a medal found in the bow of many boats

Mail Delivery to Inistrahull Island, Co. Donegal c. 1930 Note box oars

**W**ater from the 'blessed' wells such as St. Columcille's in Moville, was thought more likely to bring protection from the saint rather than relying on the dubious protection of Donegal County Council tap water! There was danger too.

*"Many's the time were nearly foundered. One time we had the ballast tied up on the towpins and us lying over to keep her up. She was down to a couple of fingers height above water"*

(John 'Jack' McLaughlin)

Food was often scarce and life ashore or at sea was not easy for the drontheim fishermen of the pre-war years. They took what food they could with them to sea and this was often little enough to sustain them. Mostly it was home-made 'scone' bread or cold potatoes and a bottle of water. The bread would be a soda farl wrapped in a piece of paper and stuck in the wearing, a bottle of water on a nail nearby. When tea was available it was carried, in the days before the thermos flask, in a

49

bottle wrapped in a woollen sock to keep it warm.

*"What you took out with you was a bit of bread, and you weren't allowed any butter. It wasn't lucky".*

(Henry Canning)

*"In Glengad we didn't put butter on it either.... but that was because we hadn't any!"*

(Barney McKenny)

*"You took nothing with you at all, well, maybe somebody would have a piece of dry bread in his pocket. There was nothing in them times, don't be talking."*
(John 'Jack' McLaughlin speaking of the 1930s when he was 17 or 18)

Danny O'Sullivan of Strove tells of a fisherman's food for the sea as:

*"seven cold potatoes, three handfuls of limpets and a bottle of buttermilk".*

## LONG LINES
Winter long line fishing sustained the fishing communities till the salmon came again in the early summer. In open drontheims in all weather, hauling by hand was cold and heartbreaking work.

*"Ye didn't to because ye wanted to, ye went because you had to."*

(Barney McKenny)

*"Long line fishing in the wintertime was wild sore on the hands, and heavy to board in the deep water. Everything was done by hand. You were just in the shakes with the cold. I mind going out in the frost and cold and it would cut the nose off ye, the cold of it, before the light in the morning."*

(Henry Canning)

Lines were maybe half a mile long with hundreds of hooks baited with mussels, 'glimma' (hermit crabs) or 'cuhorns'(whelks). Greencastle favoured the cuhorn while Glengad used mussels.

Cuhorns were caught in baited baskets and each fisherman had his own line of baskets which he baited

Fishermen at Dunaff, Co. Donegal
Courtesy J. Canavan, Moville

A Family Day out on a
Drontheim. Culdaff 1940s
Courtesy H. Tinney

Obtaining mussels for bait in Glengad often involved long journeys to collect them at Inch, Fahan Bay or even as far as Rathmullan. Hooks were also baited with lugworms dug at Trawbreaga Bay where men dug for four or five hours after walking over from Glengad 10-12miles away.

Lines needed buoy markers and before the day of plastic or glass these were made by the fisherman themselves with the skin of a dog!

*"You'd take a big useless dog that was no good. They'd make a job of him, legs, arse, and everything."*
(Bob Cavanagh)

The unfortunate animal was hanged, to avoid puncturing the skin, skinned and then cured, sewn and finally tarred. A wooden spool with a bung served to inflate the dog-buoy! The strong tides flowing off the north coast generally pulled the buoy underwater. It would then reappear as the

and set. Then the cuhorns had to be cracked open and the lines baited and carefully coiled in buckets or boxes. Mussels were carried out from Glengad in the drontheims, then opened and baited at sea. Seven men generally went to the long lines from there and four or five from Greencastle.

*"How many of them young fellas would do it now…sit down on a beam and it white with frost, take up a 16 or 18 foot pole and row away to Bealalochar. Four men and them rowing hard for an hour and a half or more, praying for a breeze o'wind and then maybe when they'd get one prayin' for it to ease till they'd get home!"*
(John Jack McLaughlin)

tide slackened at the turn. The fishermen waited until they saw the 'dog watchin' which was the time to haul the lines.

*"Them ould dogs would do nothin ....at least they're workin' now!"*

(Bob Cavanagh)

Dogs also had another function - this time alive. When boats were caught at sea in fog a dog was put in a bag and left on a cliff or harbour. The constantly whining and yelping dog guided the men home. Hard times for the family pets!

Fishing gear was largely inadequate for the demands of the work and this included the men's own clothes. Oilskins were either unavailable or too expensive. Protective clothing was often home-made from sewn-up flour bags painted with 7 or 8 coats of boiled lindseed oil, stuffed with straw, hung up and then smoked in the same way as the fish. There were not really waterproof, only keeping the wearer relatively clean. Water soaked through them.

*"You'd get nobody to do that now - go out on a frosty morning. You had to sit on that beam and it covered in pure white solid frost. Well, that ould wet damp went right up your backside through them ould oilskins."*

(John 'Jack' McLaughlin)

## SALMON

Salmon were fished at night long ago and up to recently, because the old 'barked' nets were not effective in daytime because the salmon could see them. Nets in those days were flax and knitted or braided by hand by fishermen themselves. Before they could be used they had to be 'barked' that is, soaked in a boiling mixture which consisted of tannic acid from oak bark and which acted as a preservative. Still, nets rarely lasted longer than three or four years. Sails were also barked which gave them a rich distinctive brown.

When fishing salmon all the sails were lowered and two men rowed, keeping the boat up to the net all the time. The rope from the boat to the net was called the 'swing'. The net was shot over the boat's quarter,

one man on the lead weights, one on the corks. The net was boarded with the boat's stern towards it. In John Jack McLaughlin's time the nets were the old barked flax ones which rarely held all the salmon they could have. If they got over 20 there was a bottle of whiskey for the boat!

Nets and sails had to be dried whenever possible, to avoid rotting when damp and for nets that usually meant after each fishing trip in the salmon season. Nets had to be unloaded, spread out to dry and then reloaded that same evening when fishing was done at night. Great areas of drying nets were a common summer sight on the green areas of Moville, Greencastle and elsewhere up to the late 1950s when the old nets were replaced by nylon.

*"The old nets, when you had them, were hopeless, and the ould ropes that was on them too. If they had any weight on the ropes or nets they would burst. Many's the time they did burst."*

(Henry Canning)

The only lights at sea were wooden lanterns with glass panels and a sliding door, a wooden door that lifted up… and a candle! Hurricane lamps and battery lamps came much later.

*"Fishing salmon in drontheims involved extraordinary work. The boats were run down to the water, ballast and nets put in maybe about 4 o'clock in the afternoon. Then home for a drop of tea and away rowing or sailing to the Bann mouth by 9.00 p.m. Maybe they never caught a fish, or very few, rowed back, unloaded the net,* *brought it up to spread out to dry, took out the ballast and hauled the boat. That would have been as near as dammit seven in the morning."*

(Liam McCormick)

From all the remembered accounts, while the fishing life was crushingly hard, fish were abundant. There was rarely a problem in filling a boat, only in finding buyers.

'Wee John' McCormick relates going to fish on 'Hemptons Bank' on a Friday night, a long row or sail, hauling the lines on a Saturday morning and getting a good catch, rowing back to Greencastle and finding no market. Then they rowed over to Magilligan Point to try the buyer George Leek, but no market there, then rowing on to Coleraine, no market there either, on to Portrush and finding it market day. They sold the fish off the boat and were home in time to change their clothes for 11 o'clock mass on Sunday!

This abundance lasted until and especially during the Second World War when the Fleetwood trawlers were absent. As fishing techniques advanced afterwards, the great shoals were predated and disappeared. Communities collapsed and only survived when outdated technology such as the drontheim was surpassed by the modern powered fishing boat. The sailing fishers were gone forever.

# THE DRONTHEIM COMMUNITIES:
# THE NORTH-WEST COAST
# DONEGAL BAY

*"A boat with a gurnard head and a mackeral tail."*

(GeorgeGallagher)

The western limit of the drontheim was Donegal Bay and in this area they were simply called 'yawls'. They were sailed from its many small villages such as Inver and Teelin and in the 1950s there were up to forty yawls around Inver and St John's Point. Few survived to the 1960s.

A great fishery had existed here since ancient times, but by the time of the great famine in 1847 it had greatly declined:

*"The coast everywhere affords the means of an abundant summer fishing; but the want of proper boats and tackle deters the fishermen from venturing to struggle against the stormy seas that break against the shores in winter. The fishing for codling, haddock, and glasán and that of turbot and other flat-fish, all of which are present in inexhaustible abundance, is little attended to by the neglected and discouraged fishermen."[1]*

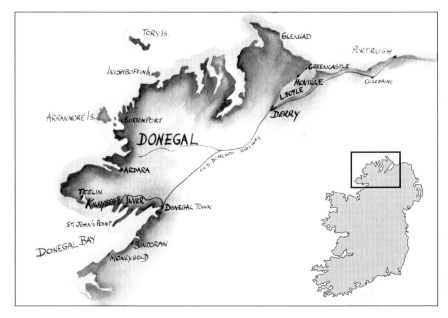

Greencastle yawls had come here in the 19th. century but most were introduced by the Congested Districts Board in the 1890s. Attempts had been made to introduce them across the Bay in Mayo but had failed, *"due to the slackness of the fishermen and the want of railway communication"[2]*

But the old west Donegal railway was run as far as Killybegs from Derry at the end of the 19th. century so yawls built at Moville or Portrush could easily be shipped that way. There was a station at Inver but men also walked to Portrush and Moville to buy them.

So successful were the yawls here that there were said to be 100 in the Donegal channel at the turn of the century, between Teelin, St John's Point, Inver, and Donegal Town. Certainly there was a great harvest of fish of every kind to be had before the trawlers of Killybegs put an end to it.

[1] " History of the Diocese of Raphoe" by Lewis 1847
[2] William Micks : "Account of the Congested Districts Board for Ireland" 1891-1923. Dublin 1925.

# BOATS

Boats were between 21ft. and 22ft. with the occasional larger 26ft. or 28ft. and again the smaller one was easier hauled on the isolated beaches.

Entries from McDonalds Register:

*March 1918*
*24 x 6-4 x 2-5*
*William McCallaig,*
*Ballysaggart, Dunkineely.*
*£20.0.0*

*September 1921*
*20 x 6 x 2-4*
*Patrick McBrearty,*
*Kilaltan, St. John's Point,*
*Dunkineely.*
*£26.0.0*

*August 1937*
*22 x 6-4 x 2-6*
*4 Oars Mast and Sprit.*
*Danny McCallaig,*
*St. John's Point,*
*Dunkineely.*
*£27:8:6*

George, Peter and Johnny Gallagher of Inver all sailed the yawls and relate that here the use of ring nets for salmon, mackeral and sprat required a yawl with particular characteristics, a high bow and stern with a 'spring to the sheer'. Curiously not unlike the original Norway model which may have come here too, generations ago. They were not to be 'flat on the run'. Hauling the ring net at sea required the yawl to lie over on her side.

*"I like a boat that's well sunk in the middle and raised at both ends. Regardless of how you filled her, you still had a head and you still had a stern. The 'sunken' boat for here was always the best boat"*
(George Gallagher)

Peter Gallagher confirms the pliability of these yawls when he relates that if an iron bucket was being carried for any reason, the one place it was never put was tight in the bow or stern,

*"In the dead-wood, in behind the stern seat because of the play of the boards.; jammed tight in there it would be liable to crack the boards"*... implying that the hull moved and flexed as the boat moved through the water.

Instead of the loose sets of laths used for flooring elsewhere, permanent laths (or 'weerins') were here nailed across the timbers on either side of the keel.

A wide, loose foot-board covered the keel and sandstroke amidships. The bung was known as a 'spile'.

## SAILS

At Inver the yawls, when fishing, carried the sprit-foresail and larger loose-footed sprit-mainsail and jib (though often without this jib, similar to the Skerries yawl). Masts were set in the 1st and 3rd beams The iron clasp or 'locket' was rarely used here for fear of snagging nets or lines. Each mast had two 'sets' or stays, tied down to the wearing or 'chock' (from the Gaelic *teac*) Stays were simply hitched or tied to a forged iron ring at the masthead. Sails were of the familiar cotton, barked red. If the weather was bad they used only a sprit-sail and a jib tied down to the stem-head. Mast positions were often changed at sea, so skillful were the fishermen at this difficult manoeuvre, especially as the mast had to go through a hole in the beam. Peter Gallagher describes the stamina and skill of the man at the sprit when there was a strong wind on the big Atlantic swells off west Donegal with a following sea. It was essential that the boat did not run too fast ahead or slide on the crest of a swell. To do so meant capsize and disaster…

*"You had to be a bloody good man to be there at that pole (sprit)….. In a big swell the man at the mast and the sprit was more important than the man on the tiller. He had his arms around the sail and dropped it,(the sprit) when they were on top of the swell to reduce her way in case she'd broach, then raised it when they were down in the swell to get her up !"*

This same dangerous but vital skill was common among the great Shetland fishermen a century ago raising and lowering their lug-sails in exactly the same manner.

## OARS

Four oars were carried. Usually a 16ft. 'bow' oar, 'middle or second bow' 18ft., 'beddin' oar 17ft. and 'after' oar 14ft.. The strongest men were on the second bow and the 'beddin' oars and in the big yawls these might be 'double-banked' (two men on a single oar). The strongest man might even take the second bow oar on his own with two men on the opposite side. As the late Jimmy McCallig of Killybegs remarked *"Rowin them double-oars was a bastard"*.

## FISHING

As elsewhere life here was dominated by the needs of the land and the coming and going of the fish. The year began with winter long-line fishing in Febuary till April or May when turf had to be cut. The salmon came in June and July and at harvest time came the 'wee fish'; the great sprat shoals as well as the swift mackeral. The herring came in September or October and lasted often till after Christmas.

## THE RING NET

The greatest catches at Inver Bay were made with the ring net (or 'dullin tram'), shot from the yawl.

The 24ft. boats carried up to seven men for the ring nets. These great circles of net were used for herring, sprat,and salmon which shoaled in the shallow water of the bay. The net was about 140yds. long and when carrying the tram the crew walked in single file about 2yds. apart, each man walking at the same pace and each bearing his share of the net on his shoulder. The net was shot from one boat as the salmon or sprat 'showed' on a bright summer's day. Buoyed at one end it was rowed around in a great circle and then hauled to the boat. An anchor out on its opposite side ensured the boat did not get pulled into the net instead of vice versa. A man stood amidships plying an oar over and back in the water with a see-saw motion, known as 'stirrin' this discouraged the fish trying to escape by swimming under the boat as the net was hauled in towards it.

*"When you closed that ring you stood up on the beam, or the 'taft',[1] one foot on the gunrail (gunwale) and you got that 18ft. oar and you put it between the ropes till the 'sole' ropes (bottom ropes on the net) came in. You never took that oar*

---

[1]This word is used in Shetland also. It comes from the Gaelic word "taibhte"for a seat or beam

time or they would rot if left in the water too long. If the nets were left out for a second night due to bad weather or such, any herring caught and left would be known as 'drowned herring' and were no good for market. In the days before proper oilskins and rubber boots it was cold work:

*"On many's a frosty winters' night*
*you tied the old oilskins round your*

*out of the water until the last of that ring would be coming in."*
(Peter Gallagher)

On a very dark night herring could be ringed by watching for the phosphorescence caused by their movements, the 'fire' as it was called locally. Instead of an oar a bag of sand being raised and lowered on a rope created a 'ball of fire' to keep the fish in the net.

*"I remember filling her once with herring, eleven-and-a-half crann. That's about 46 boxes in a 24ft. yawl on a bad night."*
(George Gallagher)

Winter herring were taken with staked nets which were anchored and left across a tide. They were about 150 to 200 yards of barked cotton which was left out at night. The 'tram' of nets had to be lifted in the morning, brought ashore when the herring would be shaken from it. They were then spread to dry each

**Carrying the Tram.**
Inver. Co. Donegal. Mid 1960s

*ankles, left your boots inside the boat and hopped out in the cold water to pull up the boat. Boats had to be unloaded of catch and ballast, hauled up on green sticks each time..... time and time again. It was all the drawin' up of the boats. That's why the boat was 24ft. You drew her up and you drew her down. It was hard. You never saw the like of it!"*
(Peter Gallagher)

Herring had always been the mainstay of fishing to the Inver fishermen and they followed them round the coast. Vincent O'Donnell of Inver relates that he heard of boats sometimes transported by horse and cart to other ports such as Ardara and even as far as Inishboffin, when the herring were plentiful there and not at home. The nets and gear were placed in the cart and the boat positioned upside-down on top. If it was a 26ft. yawl then part of the boat covered the horse's head and a very quiet horse was required. Boats were even transported by lorry across country as far as the south east coast of Co. Waterford chasing the elusive herring.

Winter line fishing was equally hard. Boats went out six or seven miles from St John's Point. Lines were up to 2,000 feet long baited with lugworm or a mackerel 'strap' (a piece cut from the silver skin on the tail).

*"Sometimes they went off in the middle of the night. Cold tea or buttermilk to drink. Their first shot would be at the break of day with a hurricane lamp beside the basket of lines. Haddock, pollock, perhaps a few ling and on the way back collect a few mussels from the beach for bait. These were brought into the kitchen and while the men eat or slept the women re-baited the lines and it was away again at maybe 5 o'clock that evening."*
(George Gallagher)

Mackeral 'drovin' took place in late summer, when waiting for the herring or sprat to enter the bay. The yawl was ballasted carefully and the sails were set so that she could almost sail herself. The sheet could almost be tied! Two lines were over the stern, two further up along her side weighted with heavy lead weights ('plumbs'). Each line had one hook baited with a mackerel strap and the shoals were hunted as the yawl drove herself steadily out into the wide bay. Perhaps a more pleasant kind of fishing than winter long-lines. *"You could get maybe ten boxes for a day's drovin' in daytime."* As boxes were filled ballast was thrown overboard to compensate.

Yawls rarely needed to venture far in Donegal Bay but nonetheless men were lost. George Gallagher's grandfather's boat coming home full of herring in 1904 'foundered in a breeze' and all were lost!

"A sad fatality occurred on Thursday night or early Friday morning to one of the crews of the Inver fishing fleet. The fleet of boats all went on Thursday evening to the Bunatrohan and Bundoran shore, and nearly all were successful in making good catches. It is surmised that that the wrecked boat must have been overloaded with herring and in coming for home across the bay was overturned by a sudden squall and turned keel uppermost, as when the broken boat was got on Friday morning at Ballysaggart, St. John's Point, the dead body of the skipper Peter Kennedy was found, his hands having a firm death grip on the keel."

Extract from the *Donegal Vindicator,* Friday, Dec. 10th 1904.

The yawls died out as this type of fishing died away in face of the trawlers in the 1950s. While an occasional ring net is still shot on the sprat at Inver the shoals and small boats have almost gone with the hard men who sailed them.

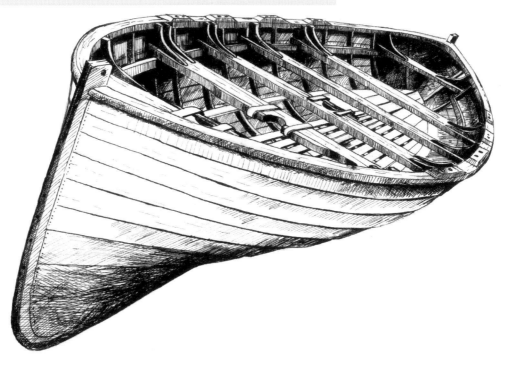

# TEELIN

Further west of Killybegs and Inver, in a Gaelic speaking area lies the village of Teelin. Yawls had been common here and Sean O'hEochaidh the Donegal folklore collector was born here. He fished yawls for five years in the 1920s. At that time there was at least a dozen yawls fishing there, all built by McDonalds and Beatties. Men from here thought nothing of sailing the boats from Moville round Malin Head, down the long Donegal coast and round into Teelin. Most boats here were 26ft and 28ft. and they carried the big 21ft. 'box' oars. There was usually a crew of seven and sails were the usual spritsail (in Gaelic *Seol mór*) and jib *(eiteog)* but with the addition of a small 'jigger' or mizen sail *(seol deireadh)* at the stern. Here also the Beattie boats were considered "*great boats, McDonald's not just quite as fine!*"

Fishing was fairly similar to much of the rest of Donegal Bay, winter long lines and the big ring-nets. Sean, a great story-teller himself vividly recounts some harrowing encounters at sea. Whales followed the great shoals of autumn and winter herring here also as the herring shoaled on great blooms of plankton, today called the 'red-tide' but in his day called in Gaelic the *meall-dearg.*

In those days of abundant fish herring were large, "*10 inches long and as broad as your hand*" Sean remembers huge catches of up to 10,000 fish (in the days when they counted the herring). But prices were as low as 5s. a thousand.. The fishermen were at the mercy of the dealers who ruthlessly exploited them.

Along with the herring came the harmless but gigantic basking shark, the 'sun-fish', *(liabháin)* trawling with its great mouth through the plankton Once going out with a ring-net, Sean and his companions found also a great shoal of basking shark and had to sit and wait for them to leave. As the wind changed the sharks disappeared. As a ring was shot one of the 40ft. monsters that was still there became entangled in the net. As the net was cut away with a scythe blade on a pole the thrashing fish stove in two of the yawl's boards. But as Sean casually put it *"They soon got them closed up with a few old coats and got home safe enough "*

A more tragic encounter was related to him in 1938 by a man called Rafter who told him of his father standing in the bow of a yawl and a whale came up out of the water taking both him and the stem of the boat in its jaws! As the men in those days didn't keep their boots on in a boat all the time, and wore homespun wool socks the last the crew saw of the unfortunate man was his brown socks disappearing in the gullet of the monster! In this case the whale was probably the more dangerous sperm whale which venture into these waters on rare occasions.

# ARRANMORE

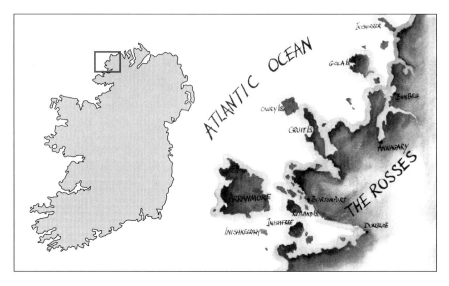

*"She is twenty feet from bow to stern and her masts are short and strong,*

*And with brown sprit-sails on her fore and main tis she can roll along;*

*With her halyards fast on the weather gun'l, and right good stays are they,*

*And a bit of a jib to keep her up in case she'd make leeway,*

*Oh! that is the rig that I would have whenever I go to sea*

*For that is the rig of the Rosses men, and it's good enough for me."[1]*

The old carvel boats here were replaced by the yawls in living memory at the start of this century. Eddie 'Bhell' Gallagher remembers the carvels as being big enough, up to 28ft.

In famine times the curragh had been the islander's only boat and the report of James Tuke, a Quaker who came to west Donegal noted in 1847, the year of the great Famine, recorded that;

*"The sea is teeming with fish of the finest description, waiting, we might say, to be caught... but their coracles were not adequate for this task and thus the people starve because they have no one to teach them to build boats more adapted to this rocky coast"[2]*

The yawls suited the islanders needs better and were still light and easily handled around the maze of islands in this area.

At one time almost every house on the island had a yawl, sometimes two, one big one and a smaller one for ring-netting. There were almost a dozen with their families on the flat and treeless Inishkeeragh. Yawls were also common on Rutland, Inishfree, Owey, Gola, Inishmean, and other nearby islands. The fine sight they made, as they tacked out of a summer's evening from the big island to drift for salmon before returning the next morning is remembered to this day.

## RIG

The yawls were large here, 26ft. to 28ft. and the fishing rig was one

[1] Off the Rosses from "By Bog and Sea in Donegal" by E. Shane (1928) Selwyn and Blount, London
[2] J.H. Tuke "The Condition of Donegal" (London 1889)

sprit-sail with boom, and jib. Sometimes a smaller second spritsail was set for a long passage or light winds. For regattas the mast had two tarred stays "*There's no give in them then*" tied down on the second beam or to chain-plates at the gunwale. Sails were calico, barked or painted with 'bluestone' to preserve them.

Boats came from McDonalds, Hopkins and Kelly by train and lorry to Burtonport. Oars were 16 to 18ft. and the half ton of ballast of large flags rested against the boats' 'second-skin'. Yawls had this extra skin of wide boards nailed along the frames below the wearing and down to the 'foot-board', a long, loose plank laid along the centre-line. This 'second skin' can be seen on the 18ft. punts on Aranmore today.

## FISHING
The heyday of the yawls here was also the time of the great herring shoals, as Eddie Bhell described the abundance, "*By Chrisht there were herrin' in them days*". In their millions they thronged the shallow waters between the island and the mainland to spawn from late August to October. They were trapped first with a drift net and then ringed within the trap. They were lifted into the yawls in baskets and the boats were often filled to capacity and rowed back with "*one board off the water*" and, of course, "*they were big herrin', not like the ones today!*"

Such were the throngs of herring in the 1780s that the landlord of the area, the Marquis of Conyngham had quays, houses and stores built on the nearby islands of Inishcoo, Rutland, and Edernish to exploit the bonanza, no doubt increasing his personal fortune but bringing some revenue to the families of the islands. The herring disappeared as quickly as they came and the fishery collapsed. The cut stone quays and roofless houses remain on the islands to this day.

Some herring were salted for home and the rest were sold to Scottish dealers at Burtonport. In the 1920s they got five shillings a basket... thirty or forty baskets to a boat, good money in those days when a 26ft. yawl cost only £35.

From McDonald's register:

*1919   26 x 8 x 3*
*Philip O'Donnell for*
*Capn. Hugh*
*Arranmore. £35:0:0*

*1920   25 x 6-6 x 2-10*
*John Early*
*Arranmore £35:0:0*

*1928   25..5 x 6-6 x 2-10*
*Coppered throughout*
*Matthew Lyons*
*Leabgarrow*
*Arranmore Island*
*£35:0:0*

Everything was fished here: lobsters in spring, then the summer salmon, autumn and winter being the great herring harvest. In the springtime sometimes long-lining was done for 'ludars' (glasán or coalfish) when bigs shoals could be found inshore. But Eddie Bhell Gallagher remembered fishing them in wintertime:

"*In frosty weather, month of January, I remember it well. Severe frost, long, long, ago; seventy years or more, the men what they used to do for heat was put down some flags of stone in the middle of the boat. On the top of the flag an old bucket. They would light a fire and every man would take his turn for heat. It was cold on the fingers. There was no such thing as rowin' about and trawlin' for them, but put a bait on the hook and wait for them. It was cruel, you know, tryin' to put a bait on a hook with the cold. That was the old system. No one would believe the hardship then."*

The same hardship was common when collecting turf or cutting seaweed. Peadar Joe O'Donnel describes the latter;

*"It would be cut off the rocks over on Inishfree, taken back by sail, unloaded off the boat by women with creels, taken by them then to the potato drills by donkey. Then me and the missus put in the seed the same evening!"*

Transporting cattle was done by putting seaweed (or wrack ) on the yawl's bottom boards to protect them, then a path of wrack was made down the pier and over the

Yawl near Iniscoo Island, Co. Donegal with "Pet Cow". Note child at its head
(Courtesy Mrs. A. Loane)

gunwale to encourage the beast. One foot was lifted in first, then the other. A 'pet' cow might stand, others had to be tied. The landlord of this area in the last century recorded an incident he witnessed;

*"Another instance of the rash and reckless daring of these islanders may be told. It happened recently in the neighbourhood. A man and his wife coming out of the island of Arranmore, in a little boat filled with turf had a horse standing on top of it. With the roll of the sea, the animal was thrown out, and as they were a long way from the land must have been drowned, had not the man cleverly succeeded in getting him into the boat again."*

How such a feat was managed is not recorded!

[1]"Facts from Gwedore 1845" Lord George Hill. (Dublin 1846)

# DISASTER

The yawls here will forever be associated with the terrible Arranmore disaster of 1935 when a yawl carrying young people back from working in Scotland capsized on the way over from Burtonport at night. 19 were drowned with only one survivor. One family lost six children, another seven. Patrick Gallagher, the only survivor, related what happened;

*"After the yawl was wrecked, nine of us climbed on her, including three of my brothers and my father. Then she overturned and pitched us into the sea in the mist and dark. There were fewer struggling in the water then, and once more I got on the keel. I remember now that Ned Ward, the bowman of the Arranmore life-boat, clutched my father Edward Gallagher, and struggled alongside the yawl holding him. He shouted 'Here is your father for you, Pat.' I got hold of my father. Not long after I saw that Ned himself was gone. When my father died after about two*

The ill-fated boat which was wrecked near Arranmore Island, nineteen lives being lost, is here as it was being recovered from the Sea.
*Irish Independent Wednesday November 13th, 1935*

*hours in the perishing cold water I could not hold him, for he was so heavy. I kept a hold of my brother Michael."*

Today there is one sailing yawl left on the island which sails against the 16ft. punts each summer now. The remains of half a great 28ft. boat lies upturned as a sheep pen at the back of the island… the last of the old yawls.

# INISHBOFFIN AND TORY

Drontheims/Skiffs on Inisboffin 1991, with the 'Clochán' in the background

*"You would never do on an island without a yawl."*

(Jimmy Ferry)

When the Gaelic-speaking population of Inishboffin was at its highest (around 200 people after the war), there were up to 20 drontheims pulled up here on the '*chladaigh*' (the island's rock-strewn foreshore) facing Magheraroarty. They were never known here as drontheims but rather as 'yawls' or more commonly as 'skiffs'. Most were 26ft. but earlier the islanders had sailed a great 28ft. boat called '*the big salmon boat*', in Gaelic '*an bád mór*'. This had a beam of 8ft. or 9ft. and oars of 18ft. It was often sailed over from the Foyle where most were built by McDonalds or Beatties. The later, smaller yawls, were mostly delivered by lorry from Derry. Some very fine ones were built by a Bunbeg man, Paddy Gallagher, who built the one now restored and sailed by Gerard Diver of Ballybrack, near Moville.

The *bád mór* had mostly fished salmon before the war, but had proved too heavy to haul on the island's steep and rocky beach and was replaced by the lighter 26ft. boat. The 26fts became the main island boat until they in turn were replaced when engines arrived in the 1940s. A 28ft. *bád mór* brought to the island by Jimmy Ferry's father from McDonalds in 1950 was magnificently restored by Brian McDonald in 1995 and has been rigged and sailed again since then by Jimmy who still spends much of the summer on the island.

Every family on the island had a boat. There were twenty-five families there one time with their own small schoolhouse and chapel. This number declined to fifteen or sixteen in the 1950s.

No one lives permanently there now, though some fishermen and their families live on the island during the summer fishing season.

The skiffs lasted much longer here as working boats because there was no safe or sheltered anchorage for larger heavier ones. Islanders could not risk their precious craft. Skiffs could be run up safely on the beach, even with a load of herring The whole island, women and men, would be at the *chladaigh* to haul the boats then. They were the lifeline of the island, used for fishing, the transport of cattle, sheep, and horses from the mainland, as well as fuel and seaweed for crops. Everything was carried in the skiff.

The last skiffs were arguably the finest ever built by McDonalds when materials were at their best. Beautifully light, with no superfluous fittings, they were superbly well-built from seasoned deal and larch planking on swept-grain oak. Tiny mast steps were laid across only the keel, garboard and sandstroke, (here called in Gaelic *'an strác beag'* the little strake). They were 'fine' fore and aft with a deep keel yet beamy and generous for cargo carrying. With the coming of the engined half-deckers the last five

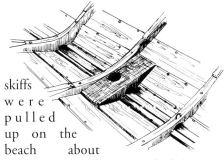

skiffs were pulled up on the beach about 1950 and tied down snugly below the little chapel as if waiting to be run down again to the sea once the winter was over. They survived remarkably well, lying here in the open since the 1950s, a tribute to their builders and their fine timber.

All but one are gone now. One was sadly burned when fuel was scarce, another broken up, but two are being restored, one by an islander John O'Brien who intends to sail it again from the island.

## SAILING
The skiffs here had a different sail-plan to the Foyle drontheims. Two different rigs were used. The first had two spritsails set on the 1st and 3rd beams.(Only these two had the long side knees for extra strength)

Bow section Drontheim/Skiff 1991

and a jib set on a bowsprit *(maide-bowsprit)* mounted on a 'saddle'. The aft spritsail was larger and carried a boom. This was only a simple pole held by a second beckit *(beoradh)* at the mast. The sail was loose-footed, tied at mast and boom's end. The boom came to slightly forward of the aft beam about 2ft. from the skipper, so his vision was not restricted. This rig was for light winds and usually for the salmon or herring fishing, the long passages as far north as the Swilly and out 'back of Tory'. The aft mast carried two

stays tied down to a beam or wearing.

The second rig consisted only of the large sprit-sail and jib and took the 'heavier' water on windy days.

The Inishboffin skiffs have only one mast-clasp which is on the first beam

nearest the bow. The other two beams have holes in their centre. Clasps were inclined to snag on herring or salmon nets.

There were no special pins or cleats for the sail sheets. These were held fast on the wearing or beam. The boom was controlled by a sheet through a block mounted from the stern. Ballast was large stones. The Tory men favoured iron but Inishboffin men swore that stones were lighter. The iron was 'dead' and didn't allow the boat to be sailed as well! Two short oars or 'pettles' (paddles) were used in rowlocks at the bow beam - for rowing when carrying a big load of turf, seaweed or herring, but also to help turn the boat's head when going about in a light wind. The long oars were 16ft.(or 18ft. on a *bád mór*) with a rounded loom.

As always the drontheim or skiff was admired for its sailing qualities;

*"She wouldn't take much water. She was fine and dry on a windy day"*

(Muirish O'Brien)

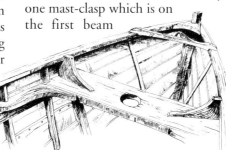
Bow Sprit 'Saddle' Bunbeg 1995

26ft Inisboffin Skiff at Magheraroarty. Now being restored, 1998.

Traditionally Inishboffin boats were mostly painted white, grey inside, and were tarred on the lower planks beneath the floors inside.

Skiffs here were usually moored offshore by the stern. A chafing board was often added at the forward edge of the aft beam with a short timber beneath for added strength. This same board and timber was also added to the forward beam along with a side - knee. The beam was thus very strong both for mooring and carrying a mast. Delicate cheek pieces were also fitted into the gunwale at the top of timbers for extra strength at the 'lifting- beam' or a rowing station.

Most boats were crewed by four men, one on each sail and one on the tiller. There was also a strong tradition here of women rowing. They were considered equal to men on an oar and often took the skiffs to Magheraroarty or elsewhere when the men were working.

Unlike an engined boat making a stormy crossing to the mainland and taking plenty of water over her bows the skiff was invariably much drier. An islander was once heard to remark on the dry-sailing qualities of the skiff;

*"If the cloth was on her she wouldn't lift a drop. (Dá mbeadh an teadach uirthi, ná dtógfadh sí deor)"*

On Inishboffin the midship floors were also planks nailed closely over the frames making, the 'second skin'. Space between the frames above this floor was then also sealed, so that herring, turf-mould, or seaweed, did not slip down and clog the bilges. The large ballast stones were then laid on this second skin.

With its half ton of ballast, little wonder the 28ft. became impractical on the island's rocky beach and was replaced by the lighter and more easily handled 26ft.

*"They could pull an oar as good as any man, some of them. They were brought up with that. Some*

*of them had to do it if there was only a brother in the house. But they were strong, strong, women. They rowed more on Gola and Inishmean. I seen us pulling a boat up half-loaded with herring and the young girls were better than the men. They would be singing and shouting. There was no such thing as hard work then."*

(Jimmy Ferry)

No people or boats are left on Gola today but by all accounts the Gola men were the best skiff sailors of all. They had Beattie boats there and these were considered slightly superior to the McDonald skiffs for fast sailing.

## FISHING

Jimmy Ferry graphically describes the life here before the island began to lose its people.

Life was dominated by the seasonal work on land and by the strong tidal flow between the island and the mainland which ran over the narrow spit connecting the two called the '*clochán*' (rocky path).

*"Rowing against the tide was the worst. Good God Almightly, many's the hard pull I seen, men rowing loaded boats between our island and the mainland, that narrow strip of water. I can tell you there's some current there. Can you imagine two men, two oars and a loaded boat down to one board, trying to break that tide (at the clochán). And that happened often. Coming that way it would be carrying wrack cut off the rocks, feamnach agus leathach!"*

(Feamnach was the short bladder wrack. Cut with a sickle off the rocks it was left to drain and then loaded into the boat; leathach was the great long tangle that lay at greater depth.)

Jimmy's brother Paddy who sailed with him described the end of the hardship of rowing when they got a little 7 h.p. engine for the drontheim. *"When we got the engine for it we thought we were in heaven!"*

In his description of sailing the 26ft. skiffs Jimmy gives us a sense of the skill and excitement involved.

**Jimmy Ferry's 'Bád Mor' and Bernard Barrs 24ft. Drontheim. McDonalds 1990**

*"Many's the time I came across just myself. Sails up and away you went to Magheraroarty. No bother at all!"*

But it was at the regattas held in summertime when sailing a *bád mór* with two sprit-sails and a jib-boom provided the greatest excitement. The half ton of ballast had to be carefully arranged to balance the boat. Ballast bags were even known to be hung up on the 'pins' to heel the boat to windward in a good breeze of wind.

*"When you're out on a boat like that you had to run from the back sometimes, even under full sail, travellin', if you thought she needed an extra hundredweight in front. You'd jump from seat to seat, at full speed, to the top, and you never thought of it. You were that used to it. The boat would tell you herself if she was too heavy behind. She'd never turn for you. As the speed goes up the head goes up. She won't go down, she'll come up all the time!"*

*I seen that bowsprit going underwater many's a time in a good breeze... and a good bit underwater... and then up again*

*and it shakin' like a leaf! And we were enjoying that. You knew what you were doin, to the inch! Every move. You were used to it all your life!*

*Anything breaking up top you just got hold of the mast and right up to the top and fixed it. No bother at all.... Ah, you were like cats, you were that used to the bloody thing"*

## FISHING

Salmon were fished in June and July. Lobster followed in August, September and into October. The once-great herring shoals came in September and were fished up to Christmas in daylight with drift nets, four per boat, 18 fathom long. At night nets could be anchored and collected in the morning. It was at the herring fishing that the whales appeared!

*"Big whales, yes. They were always after the herring. They wouldn't upset the boat. Oh, they would never touch you. They were a great sign and if you watched you knew they would make the circle on the herring; even in the daytime. She was like a sheepdog.*

*She would gather them into a 'bulk' and if you knew, and were smart and quick enough to shoot your nets outside this.... When she would make the dive she would scatter the rest and in the middle of the day you would get a boat load of herring."*

Whales mentioned here were probably *Minke* whales up to thirty feet in length which feed on herring and came in along the west coast quite close. They do 'herd' their prey into a large group, dive and come up with mouth open on the concentration of fish to take a huge mouthfull.

This was in the days of the great shoals of herring. Their disappearance contributed to the destruction of island and coastal communities all around Ireland from the Great Blaskets to Rathlin and beyond. Like the herring and the basking shark the whales have also almost disappeared.

When the herring came to Inishboffin they filled the sea between it and Magheraroarty. The same could be seen between

Arranmore and the mainland. The harvest was immense.

*"There were so many you could step out of the boat and your foot wouldn't touch the bottom. I seen three and four pound herring. They were like pollock. Eight dozen to the basket. They were the real stuff. I don't think there's many living now in the world at all. We followed them as long as they lasted..... and that was the end, herrings gone, mackerels gone, lobsters gone. Everything's taken. There's nothing left but scrap!"*
(Jimmy Ferry)

The long days of mid-winter were spent in repair and overhaul of nets, lobster-pots, and boats ready for the spring fishing of lobsters again.

*"Christ Almighty, from March on, you were up at 4 o'clock in the morning because you had to watch your tides all the time if you were lobster fishing. You had to watch for the slack, it was easier pullin'. If you waited till the tide turned a couple of hours, well, by Jesus you paid for it!"*

Seaweed was also cut as fertilizer for potatoes. Skiffs were often rowed over to Curran's Port, (about 5 miles away) for a load of turf. There was little or none on the island. One man is said to have rowed a skiff over there and back with a load by himself! Each boat took the equivalent of two tractor-loads. Jimmy Ferry describes the labour of such work;

*"Before my time there was more of it, one man going for a load of turf. When he had that boat loaded it was one board on top of the water! Then he sailed it back. They lifted it off in creels, maybe one man himself or himself and the wife.*

**The Last Inisboffin Drontheim/Skiff**
at the *chladaigh* 1997

*Dump it up there on the beach. Then fill it again and take it to the stack. Oh, talk about work! That's why, all my life I hated the bog, and the bog never seen me since."*

Seaweed was cut from the boats here also and carried great distances by oar alone.

*"They rowed to Dungloe at 4.00am in the morning and back in the evening with 'leathach' (seaweed), to be able to have time to get there on one tide and back on another in case they got no wind. They were great strong men."*

The last new drontheim came to Inishboffin in 1950 and the last working one was sailed in 1956. People last stayed all year on the island as late as 1981. In spite of government neglect and an obvious intention to rid the island of its people by providing neither basic facilities or a safe harbour islanders still stubbornly return to live and fish there each summer.

## TORY ISLAND

Skiffs on Tory Island 8 miles out beyond Inishboffin were similar. Here, in the last century they had replaced the curragh which had been used for generations. The larger boats were more common, 26ft. to 28ft. and were also painted with white lead. There might be a colour on the gunwale plank, and they were tarred inside in the traditional way below the flooring or up a couple of boards.

From McDonald's register,

1935    25' x 6'-9'x 2'-8'
May     2 Oars
        Rooved throughout,
        Cormac Rodgers,
        Tory Island.

1948    26' 7' x 2' 11'
Oct. 3  Clasps, Floorings,
        shane Rodgers,
        Tory Island.

The Tory men were admired as great oarsmen and one can only imagine the strength of these men who rowed to the mainland from here and carried boatloads of turf or seaweed back over the long nine miles of Atlantic swells. Joe Rodgers of Tory relates a story of how he and a companion were almost lost when returning under oar to the island in a skiff with a big load of turf. They were caught in a torrential rainstorm. As the turf became sodden with rain it absorbed the water and became heavier and heavier! They rowed for their life and it became a race against time to get home before the wet turf took them to the bottom or they dumped it at sea - a terrible choice. Luckily they were rescued by another island boat which had come to find them. The sea had crept perilously close to the gunwale!

Herring were ring-netted here also and as well as the whales the Tory men had also to contend with the great basking-sharks, dozens of which once cruised the western side of the island - huge timid monsters which were harpooned at Achill from currachs for their livers which produced a wonderfully fine oil. Tory and Inishboffin lamps were lit with glasán and seal oil in the days before tilly-lamp and electricity. The sea provided for many needs. A few skiffs lie rotting on Tory still and the island boats are still double-ended McDonald clinker, one or two of which began life as skiffs. Most stand idly on the shore today at Camusmore, the main harbour of the island. Beautiful, small currachs about 10 ft. are still built here as tenders for the trawlers anchored offshore.

Inishboffin and Tory are part of a completely Gaelic-speaking area and the sailing of the skiffs had its own unique vocabulary of terms and expressions most of which have passed and been forgotten though a little still survives.

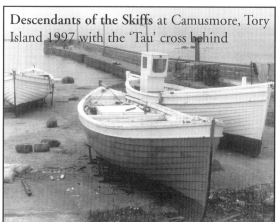

**Descendants of the Skiffs** at Camusmore, Tory Island 1997 with the 'Tau' cross behind

**The Last Tory Sailing Skiff, 1995**

# THE NORTH EAST COAST

On a spectacular cliff-top site on the Derry coast near Coleraine the 200-year old Mussenden Temple has stood overlooking a huge swath of coastline from the hills of Inishowen in Donegal, to the north Antrim coast and as far as the isles of southern Scotland. On it are carved these words from a Roman poet:

*"Tis pleasant safely to behold from shore the rolling ship and hear the tempest roar"*

They well describe these waters for it was here the Norway yawls first appeared. Their brown sails drove them for generations along this often rocky and inhospitable coast and as far as Scotland.

Engines replaced sails earlier here than on the north-west coast and almost all trace of the yawls, except some of those modified with engines and stern tubes, had been lost by the early 50s.

Although a Scottish connection has been strong here and a different religious tradition existed the fishermen of this coast formed a tightly knit community built on mutual respect and the demands of making a living on the sea along this dangerous coastline. For generations Inishowen men *'Shoneys'* had come to drift-net for salmon near the mouth of the Bann and long-lined the same seas between Donegal and the Scottish Islands. In summer time they raced at Portstewart, and the Causeway Coast men came in turn to Glengad or Moville. Religious difference counted for little in the pleasure of good sailing boats and good whiskey! These bonds of affection still remain in spite of the terrible events of recent years.

## PORTSTEWART AND PORTRUSH

An ancient relationship existed between Inishowen, Portrush, and Portstewart which centred on the fisheries of the rivers Bann, Foyle, and Roe, and their great summer shoals of salmon. For generations Inishowen men also came to the small islands off Portrush known as the Skerries to cut kelp ('*leatach*') for their potato fields and to buy drontheims in the boatyards of Portrush.

While the drontheim was sometimes known about here as a 'Skerries yawl' (so called after the small islands or 'skerries' off Portrush), by Dunseverick or Ballintoy they were called drontheims or 'Inishowen Boats'. On Rathlin they were known sometimes as a 'shallop', a term once employed to describe tenders to a man o' war during the days of sailing navies. A similar double-ended boat in Brittany is still called "une chaloupe", and the name is also used in America.

Hopkins built boats in Portush as early as the 19th century, but Moville boats built by the McDonald and Beattie families were also common. Together they built most of the north coast yawls. But the Portrush builders also produced hundreds of yawls for the fishermen of Islay, Colonsay and Cambeltown. In Scotland the yawl was known there among the Gaelic speakers as a '*Sgoth Eireannach*' (Irish skiff). Hardy Scotsmen rowed or sailed over to Hopkins or Kelly's yard at the east beach in Portrush and sailed their unpainted but linseed-oiled yawl back to Port Ellen or beyond.

Norwegian trading sailing-ships had come to Belfast, Derry and Coleraine since the mid 18th century. From 1827 Portrush became the main port for Coleraine and wood, ice and boats were often offloaded there to lessen the boat's draught before sailing up the river Bann to Coleraine. In the 19th century the timber trade changed to

**Racing the 'Big Rigs'**
Portstewart 1930s

North America and boats from Boston and Philadelphia brought the wood to Portrush. It was thus a perfect place to build boats and Portrush became the major boat-building centre on the north east coast.

It is tempting to think that the first drontheims were built here, but there is, alas, no direct evidence of this. There were yawls in nearby Porstewart in 1820 when Alexander Nimmo, a surveyor for the Irish Fishery Commission described Portstewart as:

*"…a little sea-bathing village with a few yawls, which are drawn up on the rocky shelf in bad weather; and in general the whole of the coast is unprovided with any harbour…"*

Most likely these yawls referred to were the Norwegian yawls which had once again proved their worth in working off an exposed and rocky coast. The first tiny harbour at Portstewart had only been built in 1826.

As the Norwegian trade declined and no more Norwegian built yawls came here a Coastguard officer wrote in 1836 about the yawls that were left on this stretch of coast.

*"they…are getting old, and are much patched. Two or so are nearly new. When the Norway trade existed Drontheim and Christiansand boats were introduced but they are nearly worn out, and the local people have entirely failed in imitating them. They are alike at both ends, and very low in the centre, in length about 20ft., breadth, 6ft., depth, 2ft.-4ins. The cost of this class of boat, with two lugsails, and 4 oars, is about £10."*[1]

So, by the 1830s the name 'drontheim' had already been corrupted from 'Trondheim', and while the local builders had, as he says, *failed to imitate them'* local replacments were being built which closley resembled the Norway built yawls in size, proportion, lightness and strength. The evolved design is vividly captured in a sketch by an Ordinance Survey artist, George Du Noyer in 1839. Here we can see the old worn-out Norway yawl and the new modified version with its straighter ends and up to nine narrower strakes. A yawl at sea

Portstewart.

Geo Du Noyer Delt No 1834
Co Londonderry

[1] First Report of the Commission of Enquiry into the state of the Irish Fisheries. 1837. British Parliamentary Papers.

carries the traditional two-masted drontheim rig.

## RIG

Boats were on average, 20ft. or 22ft. long, The normal 'fishing' rig was usually one or two spritsails and a jib with a crew of four. A 'gunter-rig' mainsail carrying a boom and a bowsprit was sometimes added to the normal fishing rig for regattas at Portstewart, Rathlin and Moville. Such a 'racing-rig' would have been totally unsuitable for fishing. It was dangerous enough for racing as it was. A 'dipping' or 'standing' lug-sail was sometimes used in preference to the sprit.

## FISHING

While drift netting for salmon was the generations-old tradition here there was also line fishing for pollock (lithe), cod and mackerel in the wintertime, and flatfish and lobster in the summer. Bait was mussel or lug and 'ashtray' clams called locally 'geegins' collected at Magilligan strand. The main fish buyer here was George Leek, a local MP and owner of most of Magilligan Point, including its hotel. He had a reputation as a greedy man with little under-standing of the harshness of the fishermen's lives. Later, as a Greencastle fisherman happily put it; *"His son drank Magilligan and sold off what was left of it!"*

In Portrush, where there was a fleet of drontheims at Portandoo (Port an Dhu) the lines were baited with whelks, locally called 'buckies' (the Inishowen 'cuhorn'). They were also called 'sojers' (soldiers - from their way of marching across the seabed).

But unlike Portstewart, Portrush had a fine harbour since the early 19th century and yawls could be safely moored there. However, in Portstewart the style of the boats changed and evolved much more quickly, driven by the need to fish this desperately exposed coast from a tiny and dangerous harbour.

Yawls were fine for winter long-lines and summer salmon but as trawling became ever more widespread and offered greater

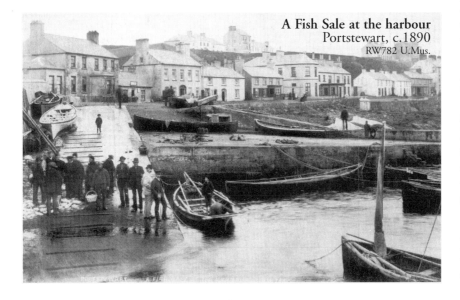

**A Fish Sale at the harbour**
Portstewart, c.1890
RW782 U.Mus.

Drontheims with Big Yacht Rigs
Racing at Portstewart c.1930s

catches, the old drontheims were raised a couple or more boards, made larger overall, with more ballast, even a small shelter-deck, and a stayed mast with a tall gaff rig with a boom. They became small sailing trawlers. Size increased to 27ft. or 30ft. and they trawled with a 'beam', a huge plank of wood used to keep the mouth of the trawl open before the introduction of otter-boards. Despite their greater proportions they were still described in the Fishery Register as 'drontheim class'.

By 1909 the little fleet at Portstewart was again transformed, this time by the introduction of engines. Some old sailing drontheims were still kept but most were engined. The old boats which survived were *held together by tar and tin."* Designs also changed, and the typical 30ft. Clinker, Double-ended, 'half decker' motor boat became as common here as elsewhere along the north. In 1999, the first new yawl for a generation was built for Portrush by McDonalds.

## REGATTAS

Fishermen from all parts of the north coast came to test the rowing and sailing qualities of their boats and men at the great regattas held at Portstewart from as far back as the 1830s. They were held at the end of the drift-net season in late August. Here the 'gentry' rubbed shoulders with the fishing folk and while military bands played selections from Wagner and Mozart men from Moville, Ballintoy, Portballintrae and Portstewart fought their hard-won races by sail and oar out in the bay.

For the races different rigs were used to increase speed at any cost. Firstly, there were always races for the 'Fishing-Rig' i.e. one or two sprit-sails and jib;

### SAILING RACE (OPEN)

**Drontheim fishing boats not exceeding 25 ft. Two sprit-sails and jib. No fins or false keels allowed. Prizes £10, £4 and £2"**

(Portstewart Regatta Programme 1925)

There was also :

### A CONSTABULARY ROWING RACE

**Four oared (open) for drontheim fishing boats not exceeding 20ft. Prizes £4, £2, and £1.**

Some races stipulated 'any rig' and drontheims now competed using yacht rigs which they borrowed locally with huge spreads of canvas which were often wildly dangerous for the crews but spectacular to watch. Of course the rigs were totally inappropriate and caused accidents and lives to be lost before being banned in later years. At one point, to increase speed, false keels and washboards up to 1 ft. above the gunwale were added to drontheims.

These 'big rigs' were raced by up to six men. One each on the two jibs, two for the main sheet and tiller and the others constantly bailing. While the ballast for fishing was round stones (which would roll out if she went over!) racing ballast was bags of gravel. On the run home for the finishing line these were flung overboard to lighten the boat.

A sailing tragedy in 1943, near the end of the sailing era when an over-canvassed drontheim capsized is related by Dan MacLoughlin of Coleraine.

*"A wee shower came and the wind came up with it and this particular boat was sailed by one of the MacMullans from Dunseverick, a Smith called 'Gunboat Smith' and a young fella called McGowan up in the bows at the jib. I think she jibed and she filled and just went down like that, like a stone, and she laden with ballast. We got Smith and MacMullan but no sign of McGowan. He was caught in the jib or between the two stays."*

That tragedy signalled the end of the regattas and sailing drontheims died out here before the war.

# DUNSEVERICK,
# PORTBRADDAN, BALLINTOY

*"These craft are generally light and easy to row. Under sail they stay without difficulty, in spite of their length, and are fast on a reach. Before the wind they run goose-winged when schooner-rigged., and they are very dry in a following sea. At Ballintoy was also a similar craft, newer and rather deeper, painted blue, with white gunwales and black bottom. She had an old donkey-shoe nailed to the lower step of the foremast, presumably to bring luck."[1]*

In 1907 it was said that there were between thirty-five and forty boats at Ballintoy most of which were yawls employing between seventy and eighty fishermen. Sammy Walkinson remembers three or four

**Thackeray in a Drontheim at the Giant's Causeway 1843**
(U.F.T.M.)

[1] Frank G. G. Carr "Notes on the Skerries Yawls". Irish Fishing Boats. Co Antrim.1932

of these boats at Ballintoy in the 80s but *"oceans of them before my time"*.

Today (1997) Sammy is one of a few of the old generation who remembers the drontheims, along with Bertie McKay of the beautifully named Portbraddan (Port of the Salmon) and Sammy Gault of Dunseverick, fishermen all their lives. In Victorian times the nearby Giant's Causeway had drawn large numbers of visitors and a favourite way to view the marvels had been by boat, mostly drontheims, and a fleet of these tourist boats (mostly 20ft.) had been pulled up at nearby Portnaboe (the Port of the Cows). One such famous visitor, the author, William Makepeace Thackeray has left us a vivid account of a drontheim trip on a north Atlantic swell;

*"After all, it must be remembered that it is pleasure we come for - that we are not obliged to take these boats. I paid ten shillings for mine, and ten minutes before would cheerfully have paid ten pounds to be allowed to quit it!*

*We were up on one swelling wave that came in a huge advancing body ten feet above us, and were plunging madly down another… before I had the leisure to ask myself why I was in that boat, with four rowers harooing, and bounding madly from one huge liquid mountain to another, four rowers whom I was bound to pay. I say the query came squeamishly across me why the devil I was there, and not walking calmly on the shore."*

(from "The Irish Sketchbook" London 1843 p.306-307)

## BOATS

*"They were easy rowed and they were easy sailed and they were great for the hard water"*
(BertieMcKay, Portbraddan)

Once again a rocky, dangerous shoreline, poor or non-existent harbours determined the size of the

**Boats at Portnaboe, c.1900**
(U.F.T.M. Wag 845)

boats here because *"it was all man-hauling on the beaches"*. 20ft and 22ft. boats were the most common, handled by four men. They were mostly called drontheims or '20fts.'

*"It was easier hauled up in the harbours. Four men could easily shift them on 'skeeds' (skids - short round poles that rolled under the keel) as they called them, up a beach."*

(Sammy Wilkinson).

25fts. or 26fts. were sometimes used for fishing drift-nets or long-lines in the winter further out around Rathlin and they used a jib and gaff-sail. A boom would be added to the gaff-sail for regattas. These were the first boats used in the old regattas. After 1929 the 20fts. were more favoured. Special large gaff-sails were kept for the regattas with washboards on the gunwales and the jib out on a bow-sprit.

The usual fishing rig at Dunseverick was a spritsail and jib but the fishing-rig in Ballintoy was never a spritsail but always a gaff-sail. Lug-sails were sometimes used at Ballycastle and Rathlin. …quite surprising diversity of rig in such a small area. This local preference for the lug-sail is unique east of the Foyle. It appears again in Co. Down and Carlingford Lough, and only on Tory island off Donegal.

Many boats around Ballintoy carried a horse or donkey shoe for luck and sometimes this was nailed to the 'step' or 'shoe' which held the foot of the mast. It greatly reduced wear and tear on the step.

**Sammy Gault and Johnny Johnstone with a very old restored Drontheim at Dunseverick, 1997**

Sails were cotton, 'Lough Neagh sailcloth' bought in Bushmills, or a very light calico of good quality. As usual they had to be soaked in bark or what was called here 'Burma Cutch' or in Ballintoy *'Catticue'* (from the bark of the Indian accacia tree, *Accacia Catechue*) bought in great lumps and melted in a drum over a big turf fire! Like the oak bark, this gave the sails their distinctive dark red colour. The hemp or cotton nets were also barked and while less efficient didn't stretch and the salmon meshed properly just back of the gills and not all the way down to the dorsal fin which happens with the modern synthetic ones. The old nets left no marks on the fish.

At Dunseverick the outside of the drontheims were always *"a red bottom, varnished top and a green stroke."* Inside they were tarred below the flooring and sometimes tar or grey paint up to the gunwale.

*"In the early days they were always tarred 'cos it was cheap. They were tarred with a sock or the sleeve of a gansey instead of a brush!"*

(Sammy Wilkinson)

Boats coming from Kelly's yard at Portrush were often painted first with sulphate of copper (the old 'bluestone' used for potato blight ) an excellent wood preservative and primed with either red or white lead, when it could be had. Here and elsewhere before boats were launched after being built or being out of the water for a long time they would be completely submerged at low tide. This swelled the timber and sealed leaks. They might also be part filled with fresh water on land(rain water even better) to 'stench' them quicker.

## OARS

Oars were usually 14ft. to 16ft. on a 20ft. boat, while the 25ft. carried 18ft. oars. At Ballintoy every man used to get his own oars made specially by one family, the McIntyres, who were not only full-time fishermen but also carpenters. Their oars were always well-balanced. Silver spruce was the best wood. During the war hickory was washed ashore but of a hickory oar Sammy Wilkinson said, *"It would take a horse to pull one of them."* One local man who tried to pull one said it was *"a good oar but it reminds me of a tree with the branches cut off it".* Ash was sometimes used but this also was very heavy. The 'rowth' here was called a *'clamper'.*

Two smaller 12ft. oars called 'pettles' were sometimes used by one man in the bow thwart for keeping the boat moving when long-lining or through creels, or keeping the boat up to the fishing 'marks', here called 'mees'. They preferred not to have a mast clasp here as *"It would take the backside of ye"* and was taken off when rowing.

It was the superb shape and handling of the double-ender that made it so perfect for these waters. The men operated in amazing conditions. The flat calm night was no good for fishing salmon. The livelier the sea the closer the salmon run to the surface. Men could go out in a wind force 5 or 6 with a light boat and a light net, but after a night's drifting with quite a few salmon and a wet net it could be a problem coming ashore. Bertie McKay describes the confidence men had in the drontheim;

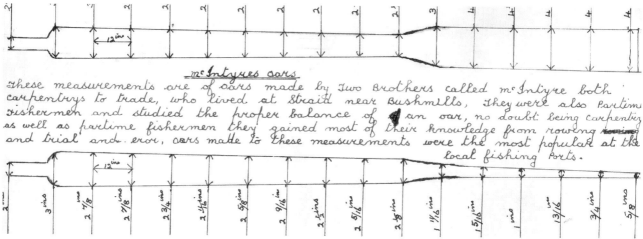

**Old oar measurements drawn by Sammy wilkinson, Ballintoy**

*"The drontheim fishing boat was the only answer running in from the sea. All these inlets, most of them were exposed to the west and you were running before seas approaching a landing which is the worst possible way to approach it. The fine end splits the sea. You could still control them. The transom-stern can be a problem unless you have some kind of decent shelter."*

Sammy wilkinson also confirms the sailing qualities of the drontheim. The double-ender here had to negotiate the powerful tides that swept like a white-capped river along this coast. They are called the 'Carraig' which flows east to west and the 'Gore', the flood-tide, west to east. All this combined with openess to the north Atlantic swells and a north-west wind blowing on to the rocky black basalt beaches made this no coast for the stupid or faint-hearted.

*"In this part of the world they preferred the drontheim's sharp stern and bow. After a follwin' sea it went past it. If it was a transom stern a sea could hit it and pushed her on. You couldn't steer and would have broached her. If you were going through a big lump of a sea a clean boat will slide through it. You want nice lines from bow to stern and a steep bilge. She catches the water and holds her ground when leaned over."*

# FISHING

As elsewhere the drontheims here were used to fish longlines in the winter, for cod, conger-eel and skate. As the cod went to shallower banks they were caught with hand lines till the salmon came in June. Long lines were carried in three baskets holding forty-five score (900-1000 hooks). Lines were preserved with Archangel tar mixed with creosote. Prices were low, Sammy Gault describes how, in the week before Christmas 1937 his boat had 71 dozen haddock and 14 big cod. £7 was asked for them, but there were too many fish on the market then. They received £3:10 shillings, which worked out at 1s a dozen for the haddock and 14 cod into the bargain!

Bait for the lines were mussels, at 2 shillings a bag from Farrens of Moville, who shipped them to Portstewart. Some even had to come from as far as Belfast Lough doing away with much of the mens' profit, even more if the weather kept them from fishing and the bait rotted. They also baited with buckies taken with creels on a bank off Bengore Head called the 'Buckie Bank'.

There were plenty of fish in those days till the trawlers arrived, cleaned out the local fishing grounds and put and end to the long lines.

# CREELS

Here, as in Inishboffin, Rathlin, and elsewhere fishermen made much of their own equipment, such as oilskins, nets, lines and creels. At Ballintoy and Rathlin creels were made with hazel but even whin (gorse) was used. This unlikely wood actually got harder in salt water and when carved into a net needle and soaked in linseed oil became supple and strong. Oilskins made from flour-bags or old sail-cloth were soaked in boiled linseed

The Gault brothers, Dunseverick. George, Sammy, Bob with 'Buckie' creels 1961 (U.F.T.M.)

oil mixed with the raw yolk of an egg to give them a yellow colour.

*"But your arse still stuck to the beam when you sat down"*
(JohnJack McLaughlin)

The same oil preserved the timber of the boats. Another oil, from the black pollock *(or glasán)* also had widespread use as a treatment for muscle pain, both for man and beast! In earlier times it had been used in tanning leather. Oil from the fat of the conger eel, boiled and strained had a similar curative effect, especially for ailments in horses' hooves - if one could stand the smell! Seal oil was valued as well.

Seaweed or 'tangle' was cut from the rocks here also, but only to cut the edible 'dulse' off it. The seaweed then grew again and this growth was often washed ashore and collected after a storm to put on the fields. It was called 'The May Fleece'.

*"There'll be nae May fleece till the sea gets rough, should that be the month a July !"*
(Sammy Gault.)

## RING NETS

At Ballintoy a type of ring-net, or draught-net was used for the shore fishing of *glasán* and herring, once again in the time when fish were plentiful and large,

*"before the war when the seas were hoochin with fish"*
(Sammy Wilkinson.)

*A 'sighter' would spot the glasán or herring 'lumpin' i.e. going into a deep, large shoal on a summer's evening. A good sighter could even tell the number of fish. The net was usually run out from the shore by a drontheim around the shoaling fish, and the completed 'ring' pulled on shore with the boat at its back. The net might also be shared with the Rathlin folk and the catch divided. Sammy described this good relationship;*

*"They were all one family along here!"*

## SALMON

But it was the great salmon-run along this stretch of coast that gave the greatest harvest. Bag nets had been anchored off here since medieval times and can still be seen there today. The salmon caught here in the last century were often sold to the big fishing smacks which had come, round from Sligo and Westport (since the 1880s) laden with salmon for the English market and racing for a £5 prize for the first to reach Liverpool. It was a four days' round trip with up to 100 boxes of fish. Arriving off Portbraddan they were in such a hurry they wouldn't even stop to take on the salmon but a line was thrown, the drontheims came alongside and transfer was made on the move. The O'Rourkes of Ballintoy also transferred barrels of crabs in the same manner. They arrived at Billingsgate earlier than today.

Tragedy occured during this dangerous manoeuvre long ago when a drontheim was turned over and all her crew lost. A similar tragedy happened when a boat capsized in the last century when taking ice from one of the Norway ice boats. After this the local landlord at Portbraddan had a great ice-store cut out of the hill behind Bertie McKay's house. A river above was dammed and when the winter frost turned it to ice this was carted and passed by ramp into a trapdoor on the roof of the cave. It is there to this day, evidence of the colder winters of another century.

When the salmon shoals were still great the fish were of great size back in the 1930s and 1940s. Today a 'spring fish' is about 18 to 20 pounds. In Bertie McKay's day they were 30 or 35lbs! He remembers Bann fish of up to 43 lbs! Each year these salmon make the great journey back across thousands of miles of Atlantic to return to the river they began life in. Fish were differently marked according to their river of origin. Bann fish were short and deep with a bluish tinge, those from the river Bush were darker and smaller with a fine head and tail ....like a Beattie boat.

Farmers here didn't always make their living from farming alone and did some fishing as well:

*"The shout would have gone up 'The mackerel's in!' The horses were put in, the scythe was put down and everyone went down to the boats and out to the mackerel. Those days there were terrific shoals of herrin' and mackerel".*

(Arthur Mc Elnay)

Some fishing would be done after their crops had been put in early in springtime, when the peat had been cut and also after the harvest. There was little fishing in wintertime. Some farmers might buy a boat together and it was held in partnership between neighbours. This was called a 'company boat'. Bertie McKay tells a story of one:

*"There's a story told that goes back possibly over a hundred years to an era when the tenant farmer on the coast had his own fishing boat but there were some crews never graduated to possessing a boat of their own which meant that they were dependent on the good will of their neighbour. So invariably that*
*neighbour went out at the slack of the tide to haul lines or shoot lines or what have you. And invariably when he came ashore the tide was not terribly favourable for the other crew borrowing the boat. However, they still had to go. This story concerns one particular gentleman who was a member of the crew that had borrowed a fishing boat. It was in the month of February and they were shooting lines away off in the northwest here and it was a bad morning. The wind was hangin out of the west, sleet and snow showers and suddenly the wind came away very fresh and they had to cut their lines and fly for home, under sail. This gentleman was wont to sit up on the for'aard beam suckin' his clay pipe. Suddenly there was a very fierce gust and the boat broached. The cox'n shouted up; 'Tom, Tom, come back quick, she's gan te go doon!' Tom just looked round over his shoulder and he says 'Let her go hell, sure she's not ours anyhow!'".*

## ENGINE

The first engine appeared at Portbraddan around 1912, and at Dunseverick and Ballintoy about 1914. The drontheim converted badly. The early light engines were not so bad but later the heavier horse power destroyed the naturally evolved qualities of the sailing yawl.

*"Under sail she was good, head to wind or runnin'. See, whenever they put the engine in you had to watch her all the time when you were runnin' before the sea. Nowadays with the bigger horsepower and bigger propellor it sucks the stern down."*

(Samy Wilkinson)

Eventually the engine vibrations shook the lightly-built drontheims apart, often starting with the sandstroke, only nailed as it was to the keel. Engines required a heavier, differently built boat and the light yawl disappeared.

# RATHLIN ISLAND

*"There's no such men now. They would make two of you, big men with beards. They hadn't oars like you have. They had spars, and two hand-grips cut in them with an adze. They were the oars the Rathlin men used them days."*

(Dan McQuilkin 1953)[1]

Rathlin lies some six miles off Ballycastle on the north east coast and the tight little community here was well served by the Norway yawl for generations. There had been a Viking settlement on Rathlin in the 9th. century. Here the yawl was called a 'shallop'. While having to contend with the same rocky coastline on its northern side, Rathlin had a fine natural harbour at Church Bay. Beyond that, between the island and Ballycastle lay the treacherous tideway known in ancient times as the Sea of Moyle. A Rathlin man was asked once what

Rathlin Islanders c.1910 R. Anderson collection. U.F.T.M.

[1] "Rathlin, Island of Blood and Enchantment" Michael J Murphy. Dundalban press. Dundalk 1987

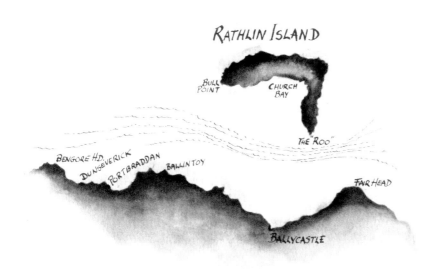

RATHLIN ISLAND

BULL POINT
CHURCH BAY
THE "ROO"
BENGORE H.D.
DUNSEVERICK
PORTBRADDAN
BALLINTOY
FAIR HEAD
BALLYCASTLE

Islanders went to Moville for boats after Kelly stopped building and here the Beattie boat is described by Loughie McQuilkin *"They weren't as 'able' a boat. They were lower, shallower, hadn't the same distance from the heel (keel) to the gunwale".* Jim McFaul another fisherman described them *"They were good and low for sneakin' under the wind".*

## RIG

The fishing rig here was also spritsail and jib but for the regattas they used a gunter mainsail with boom, spritsail and a jib carried on a bowsprit. The gunter was larger than the spritsail and was carried on a bigger mast. Again, a wildly dangerous excess of sail for a small open boat with little keel, but providing the speed and excitement that made the regattas so memorable.

## OARS

On the 22ft. boats the oars were generally 12ft. to 14ft. and rounded. Two 'pettles' were also carried. These were shorter, lighter, 11ft. to 12ft. oars. They were usually used

he thought hell was like and he replied *"If it's any worse than Rathlin sound in an ebb-tide and a nor'west wind, God luck to ye".*[2]

As on the Causeway Coast, boats here before and after the war were generally 20ft. and 22ft.. An islander who sailed them, Loughie McQuilkin describes them;

*"They were very safe boats. Though they were small they were safe and under sail they were fine and dry."*

Before the 1930s there had been bigger 20ft. to 28ft. boats but the smaller boat was favoured, again for the ease of pulling it up on rocky beaches or the numerous small ports around the island. Most boats came first from Portrush.

*"Kelly's were deeper, better for sailin'. They had a fine sharp bow, good shoulders, good bearins below. Kelly built an abler boat than Hopkins."*

(Loughie Mc Quilkin.)

[2] *ibid* P53

by one man on the for'ard beam to keep the boat up to a line or mark when fishing or were used to pull the boat's head through the wind. With its long keel the yawl can be slow to come round in light winds;

*"The keel was so light you needed half an acre to get her round a buoy! …the side drift was so tremendous".*

(Arthur McElnay)

A pettle (short oar) might also be used to help keep the boat's head up to windward.

*"One day I was out with my father coming out from the Roo going up to the Bull with a south wind and he told me 'Step the mast, sprit the sail and give her the jib. Now put a wee dab of the pettle on that side to keep her up.'"*

(Loughie McQuilkin.)

## FISHING

Usually two men, or three at the most, fished the 20ft. boats, going after lobster, crabs, and shellfish for which they made their own creels, usually during the winter months,

from hazel rods cut in October on the mainland in Glenshesk. Creels were sometimes made from whin here also. (Sammy Wilkinson of Ballintoy still makes beautiful net needles from whin which are more supple and smooth than the modern plastic.

Farmers there were happy to see the hazel and whin cut and gave permission in return for a few salted fish sent over from the island.

Lobster fishing usually began around March 17 (St. Patrick's Day) and might continue, if the weather was good, up to Christmas. Long lines were also fished with 500 or 600 hooks on a cotton line. *"In those days there were plenty of fish, no trawlers…. and a big demand!"*

A curious demand also during the war was for the dulse which the fishermen here also cut from the

'tangle' (long dark seaweed). It was dried, sold, and sent to Belfast where it was used, not for eating, but for packing artillery shells! They got 5s. a stone for it. Wartime also provided a huge market for local seabirds, all kinds, which went to feed Allied soldiers in England.

Mackerel were fished in summer with feather 'jigs' but salmon, strangely enough, were never fished here. November to Christmas saw the great draught ring-nets take huge numbers of *glasán or lithe* (black and white pollock) when hauled from the beaches. These big nets were fished by men of three or four townlands at a time as well as men from the mainland around Ballintoy.

The net was coiled into a shallop. One end was rowed out about 200 yards and back to the shore to make a 'ring'. The boat then returned to

93

the back of the net and the 'sole rope' (from the bottom of the net) was held to keep the net even as it was hauled back on shore. It was sore work.

*"The young men today are too lazy to draw in a net. You'd have to be up to your chest damn near in water hauling it. No one would do that now."*

(Loughie McQuilkin)

Long ago commands to the men on shore from the boat were often called by the old men in Gaelic. 'Tarring fe hure' *(Tarraing faoi thuaidh)* 'Pull the north end' or 'Tarring fe eastern' *(tarraing faoi theas)* 'Pull the south end'. There would be great quantities of *glasán*, 'hundreds of hundreds'. Fish were counted in hundreds then. Loughie McQuilkin recalls getting 'two hundred hundreds' 20,000 fish, off the beach in the 1930s. They were then taken to Ballycastle and sold for 1s. a hundred. At home they would be de-boned and salted like herring for three or four nights, then spread on walls to dry. Later they were brought in to the house, tied back to back over bamboo rods

stretched across the roof. When dried, they were packed in boxes. "That was your bread and butter all winter."

The melt (liver) of the *glasán* when removed and allowed to rot and ferment in a barrel produced that fine oil which had so many uses such as waterproofing the home-made calico oilskins, for treating muscular ailments but especially for burning in the little *'cruisey'* (or cruiscin - Gaelic for jug) lamps with a rush or piece of cloth for a wick which gave light by the open firesides long ago. The small pan inside the lamp for the oil was called a 'sliggin'.

*"Glasán oil was good for a rub of some complaint. It was good for a horse with colic or indigestion. If you dressed iron with it too, it would never rust."[1]*

Seaweed for fertilizer was never cut from the boats here as enough was washed into Church bay for the farmer's needs. Everything else was carried to and from Ballycastle by boat - from fresh produce and animals to ploughs and coffins.

Animals were easier handled than one might think. Two cows could be carried to Ballycastle in a 20ft.. A cow or a horse would stand on a 'floor' of bags of gravel and straw.

*"You just took the horse standin'. They might put a coat over its head and walk it into the boat from the pier. When the boat would roll the horse's nose would be in the water and when she'd roll back his tail would be in."*

(Loughie Mc Quilkin)

**'Cruisey' Lamp. Rathlin**

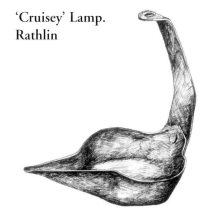

[1]. ibid, Murphy

**Islanders manhandle a horse into a shallop at Church Bay 1950s**

Courtsey L. McQuilkin

Regatta, Rathlin Island.          28.

**Shallops racing at Rathlin 1950s**
(Courtesy Tommy Cecil)

# REGATTAS

One might have thought fishermen had enough of rowing and sailing in their way of life but they loved regattas and pitting their skill against men from rival parishes. On Rathlin the regatta was held in mid-July. As well as races with the 'fishing rig', i.e. sprit-sail and jib which couldn't be changed, there were also rigs for the big 'racers', a huge Bermuda mainsail and jib. This rig was kept only for racing and was stored away in winter, along with special 'spoon' oars for the rowing races.

The boom on this big sail hung over the stern and there was a ring bolted on to the stern for a block on the sheet. Two men were at the stern of a racing shallop, one man facing aft holding the end of the sheet which came through a block from where it was anchored through a hole bored in the 'crook' (the lower part of the oak timber) or on a ring on the curve of the stem or 'skeeg'. The man on the tiller only had to steer and he gave the command whether to slack or tighten the sheet.

ibid, Murphy page 34

There was fierce competition at the regattas and it is related that in the old days there was a woman who used to make a charm to ensure her son would win! *"It wouldn't do to talk about it but she went round the boats before they started and she wore a red shawl and would throw a red wool thread into the other boats competing against her sons."* The old magic put to good use.

Loughie McQuilkin's father used to borrow a boat for fishing to let his own dry out a month before the regatta. *"Used every day for fishin' she'd be sort of heavy. It was dead serious."*

Here, it seems, washboards were allowed, and the bowsprit was held abaft the stem by a 'bowsprit-beam' or 'saddle' across the gunwale. An eyebolt was through it and a metal 'horse' fastened over it. The bowsprit passed one side of the stem-head through an iron ring bolted through it.

Damage to a wooden boat could sometimes be more easily repaired than to a modern one. Danny Hannaway relates how, just before a regatta a ballast stone was dropped and split a floor board. The boy culprit was told *"Get a spade and get up there and get a scraw"* (a sod of grass and earth). The board was hammered back, the scraw put over the board, a stone on top of it and the boat went on to win the race.

## ENGINES

Engines came to the island boats in the 1930s and were fitted to existing drontheims. On Rathlin the 'conversion' to power appropriately enough was started by a clergyman, the Reverend Brown, a former engineer. He bought old Austin 7 car engines from Belfast scrap yards for £3 or £5 and converted them for marine use. The sternpost was reinforced with a fitted block deadwood and together they were bored for the propellor. The whole arrangement somewhat compromised the soundness of the boat aft and only worked while the engine power remained minimal. So the islandmen would often *set a wee sail as well, to give the engine a bit of a boost, get a bit of speed on"*. Now at last the islanders could break the strong tides between Rathlin and Ballycastle whenever they wished. The early engined shallops carried a standing lug-sail some times in preference to a spritsail. The old engines were rarely as completely reliable as sail or oar. Some old men refused ever to go without their sail, even with a modern engine. No shallops are left in Rathlin today (1999).

## SUPERSTITIONS

*"They say the sea is always searching for someone to take with it ; there's not a tide that flows up the beach but would like to take someone with it, drowned, they say. That's what I heard now. The ocean searches out people and the old people long ago used to say that the ocean was St. Patrick's graveyard."* [1]

As in all fishing communities in the old days there were superstitions. Rathlin was no exception. In our more rational and sceptical age most of these have died out but they mark the end of generations of inherited customs and beliefs which were, and some still are, deeply important among the people of isolated communities everywhere. As with so much of western culture the watershed seems to have been the generation before the Second World War, from whom wonderful legends, folklore, and stories have been recorded.

The most common superstition seems to have been that a boat was never turned against the sun. We can only imagine the pagan antiquity of such a fear. No one ever whistled on board. Red-headed women, of course, were a disaster and men turned on their heel when meeting one and would not go out. Dan Lafferty of Moville related the story of a family there who had a red-haired child. All during the salmon season she stayed in Derry because any fisherman meeting her would turn back and not go out!

White stones could not be used for ballast here, or anywhere on the whole coast and even on Islay! A boat could not be launched with its mast already in place. Forgetting something on the way to fish, a man could never turn back without risking terrible luck.

While some superstitions were taken lightly there were more that were deadly serious….

If a boat was in trouble a knife might be thrown over to avert disaster, called 'throwing in the steel'. But the man calling down this

[1] "Stories of Sea and Shore" Irish Folklore Commission Dublin 1983

help could never go to sea again. His luck was used up! A coin, holy water, a lighted coal thrown in could also help. Tory fishermen always keep in their boats some blessed clay from the island, and this they throw into the sea to protect their boats when in danger.

Perhaps the strangest custom was keeping a small box of earth on board in case a body was ever found at sea. Then a little earth was sprinkled on it, as a priest sprinkles earth on a coffin, before it was brought aboard the boat. It was a terrible risk to take back from the sea that which it had taken. The finder of the body might be the sea's next victim. 'The sea must claim its own.' Thus in former times a crew might hesitate to recover a drowned man.

John Gillies Bowmore, Islay  c.1930
(Courtesy J. McFarlane)

# ISLAY

# "An Sgoth Eireannach" - The Irish Skiff

AMF 1905

To the north-east of the Foyle, beyond the Giant's Causeway and Rathlin, standing on the horizon, often magically close on a clear summer's evening, is the Scottish island of Islay. It has its own association with the Norway yawls.

Islay is a rocky jagged island thrusting southwards towards the north coast of Ireland Her fishermen, many still Gaelic-speaking, have shared the same waters with their Irish counterparts for a thousand years. For a time they shared also the Norway yawl.........

On a flat rock near an ancient anchorage on the east site of Islay called *Pol na h-Eala* (the 'swan's pool' in English) there is a crude carving of a boat with a broad mainsail and jib. Alongside are the initials 'A M F 1905'. Boats like this were anchored here long ago. They were locally called in Gaelic 'sgoth-eireannach' or 'Irish skiff' by the many island fishing families who sailed and rowed them for generations. Strange as it may seem, all were built in Ireland, at Portrush and Moville.

All the old skiffs are gone now, save for an ancient relic, the 'Catherine', built for Donald McFarlane in 1910 by James Kelly of Portrush and now at Portrush. The Swan's Pool lies empty and bleak now while its little jetties, once carefully maintained by the Livingtones and McFarlanes, Russells, Andersons and Campbells, crumble with each Atlantic gale.

But how did they come to Islay? The little carving was done by Archie McFarlane whose great-grandfather had come fishing here from Co. Antrim in the 1840s and had stayed and married into the island. Many other migrants had

come here over generations seeking better fishing and a better life, apparently bringing their skiffs with them.

It was old Archie's grandson, Jim McFarlane of Port Ellen, who had sailed and fished with his grandfather in the last days of the skiffs in the early 1950s who, in 1996, brought back to Islay the first new Irish skiff to have come here since then. The McDonalds of Moville, who had built it had ancient ties with Islay. The Gaelic clan McDonald, 'Lords of the Isles' had their central stronghold in the castle of Finlaggan on Islay.

The story of the Irish skiff here is told by Jim McFarlane.

The north Antrim coast and Rathlin are closer to Islay than much of the Western Isles. It would seem that the little Norse boats arrived on Islay via Ireland's north coast, sometime in the early 19th century, and not directly from Norway, as happened with the other Scottish islands. They were also enthusiastically adopted here by the fishing communities to the extent that at one time their numbers were counted in hundreds.

It was relatively easy to row or sail from Islay to Portrush and return with a skiff on the same day. But it was not a journey for the weak. The passage is dominated by strong tidal flows and could be treacherous and heart-breaking. Going to Moville was much further so most of the boats came from Portrush.

What had the fishermen used on Islay before the 1800s? Little is known apart from a legend related by Jim McFarlane

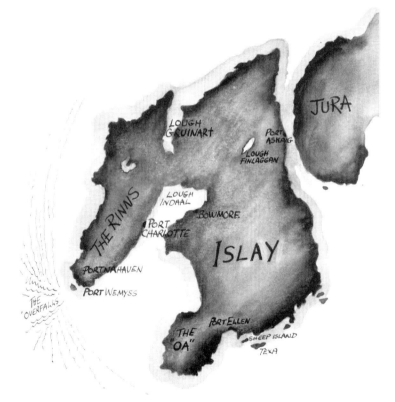

which attests to the poverty of the fishing folk over a hundred years ago. His grandfather had told him that the Irishmen who arrived here in the 1800s had described coming into Islay and finding the old boats of the fishermen:

*"The poor boats that they were moored with heather ropes; ("Bha na batan bochd a bha aca ceangailte le ropa fraoch"....) The same ropes they used to hold down the thatch on their houses."*

It would seem that there was no indigenous boat-building tradition on Islay, neither wood nor the skills necessary to built this kind of boat. But they could be relatively easily had from Ireland.

Latterly, of course, some were built on Islay by for instance, old Gilbert Clark, of Port Charlotte, who built up to the 1950s, but no distinctive design evolved here, though, as we shall see, the boats here did have features not seen elsewhere and reflected the needs of the fishermen as they evolved their own local version of the ubiquitous Norway yawl.

There were amateur builders, of course. Fishermen built their own if they could not afford to bring one over from Ireland. These were mostly built 'by eye'. Boats were sometimes uneven as a consequence and sailed well only on one 'good' side. Few, if any, could equal the boats of Hopkins, Kelly or McDonald.

In size the early boats on Islay were mostly 26ft.-28ft. with a beam of 6½ft.-7ft. and 2'3" - 10" in depth. Similarities with Irish boats can be seen from a comparison between Scottish and Irish boat records. For example,

*"ST BRIDGET." CN131. MALCOLM MCNEILL, PORTWEMYSS, 25K, 26'.8"OA, 6'.2"B. 2'.6"D. 1.94NT. 5MEN. BUILT 1905, MOVILLE. Register of Fishing Boats, Campbeltown District.*

*SEPT. 1915. NED MCLAUGHLIN, GLENGAD, CO. DONEGAL, 26 X 6-10 X 2.9. 4 SPAR OARS. 2 PLANK OARS. MAST AND SPRIT. £16:0:0.Register of McDonald Boat builders, Moville, Co Donegal.*

This large 26ft. boat was typical on Islay at the time of the great handline and herring drift-net fishery on the Mull of Kintyre at the end of the 19th century, and later these boats hand-lined the dangerous edge of the 'overfalls' west of the 'Rinns', the western headland of Islay (An 'overfall' occurs where the strong tidal current meets an underwater barrier and is thrown up in violent motion

## BOATS AND RIGGING

The Irish skiffs here were built much as they were in Ireland but with some interesting local variations. They had, for instance, a very distinctive straight 'heel' (or lower sternpost) which does not appear on the yawls elsewhere. Curiously, this is also a distinctive characteristic of the great highland galleys that sailed from here in the 15th. and 16th. centuries.

The stemhead was always high, at least 4ins. if not more, to take a bow-sprit 'saddle'.

The fishing-rig was the single sprit-sail (*seòl-spreòid*) and jib, though a second sprit-sail might be set for a long passage. On Islay 'standing' lug-sails were used for

The earliest record there is of a skiff on Islay is from the Campbeltown Register for 1880. It records a skiff 'Lily' 24' Keel, 25' 8" O.A. Built for Donal McNeill of Port Wemyss by McDonalds of Moville.

more easily hauled on the beaches and when used for lobster fishing were more easily manoeuvred among the gullies, stacks, and rocky islets of this turbulent coast. Rigged with the simple, yet efficient spritsail and jib, they were easily handled by their crew of three, were extremely fast on a reach and under oars were capable of being rowed over great distances, as some crews discovered as they met flat calm on a

## THE "22FTS."

The early large boats built for fishing the Mull were later replaced by smaller 20 or "22fts" which were

ROTHEL VALLEY 11TH CENT CARVING

regattas but were considered much too cumbersome for fishing. The spritsail, on the other hand, with the minimum of spars and rigging, could be raised or lowered very quickly, when needs be. It was simple, efficient, and easy to use.

Oars were 14-16ft. on a 26ft. and 12-14ft. on a 22ft., with a rounded section, often leather-bound, and rowed between two oak pins.

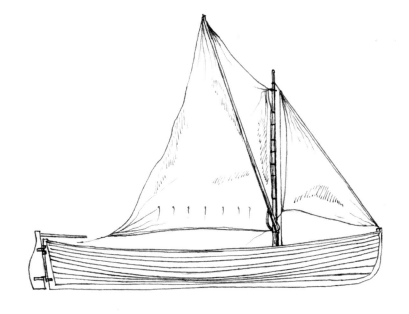

trip to pick up a new boat in Portrush or bring dried fish to Ballycastle's August Lammas Fair.

On Islay, skiffs were beached at Portnahaven and Port Charlotte but in Port Ellen were moored in the beautiful Swan's Pool behind the 'Ard' (high ground) south of the town. The boats were tied just off the small jetties owned by the families who had the skiffs.

## BALLAST

Skiffs carried ballast of fist-sized, flat round stones gathered on 'Eilean nan Caorach' (Sheep Island) opposite the Swan's Pool. They were carefully chosen... no white ones of course! and carefully placed on the floor boards... never on the boat's 'skin' and 'settled in' with smaller rocks to bind them and keep them from rolling about. They made a wonderfully stable 'floor' on which to stand. If the boat were capsized the round stones would roll out and the boat could stay afloat.

## RIGGING

The working fishermen here, as elsewhere, had little time for the romance of sail, and avoided tacking as much as possible:

*"They invariably rowed to a suitable place and then raised sail, maybe in the lee of an island or rowed to a good position to get a good tack, or well to windward to get a good broad reach, to take full advantage of the wind... so they hadn't to mess around with tacking:"*

The Irish-built skiffs, popular on Islay because of their shallower draft, could not match the Scottish-built Lough Fyne skiffs to windward in a race, even when rigged with a big lug-sail. But as old John Campbell, a skiff sailor of the old days eloquently put it, the Irish skiff had other ad-vantages:

*"She was never great at tacking but, by God 'Bheir dhith traoigh'- give her a foot of sheet and nobody could catch her. Off*

*the wind with a bit of slack (on the sheet) by God she would go!"*

Unlike the older heavier boats the "22 fts" were easily rowed and in light winds both oars and sails could be used at the same time :

*"In very light conditions all sails were set and they put two oars on*

"Catherine" racing 1930's

*the windward side, the sail counterbalancing the other side.. Just a little list on her to lift the windward bilge out of the water and away we'd go like hell."*

Jim recalls as a child his excitement as he sat on a rocky stack overlooking the entrance to the Swan's Pool and watched the skiffs coming home :

*"I loved to hear the sails flapping. The skiffs came charging in from the the open sea, flying up to the mooring. The sprit came out of the snotter at the bottom, the foot of the sprit was shot over the side, slid through your hand until you came within a foot of the top and then you held it.... It was allowed to trail behind the boat. It was easy to board it then."*

## CONSTRUCTION

The skiffs for Islay built by Hopkins and Kelly were almost identical to those built by McDonalds, but with differences which emphasised both the superb craftsmanship of James Kelly and the different requirements of the

Islay fishermen. We can see these in the old 'Catherine' She is built incredibly deep and 'fine' (i.e. having a sharp, narrow bow with steep bilges). She was built, as Jim puts it, 'as a sailing machine' with a deep-keeled 'V' hull and a distinctive Islay straight 'heel', to give her a better 'grip' in the water. This deep section can be seen most clearly where her garboards meet the sandstroke - that strange Scandinavian feature unique to the Norway yawls in Ireland. Here it is called the *'Fliuch-Bhórd'* ('wetboard' in Gaelic).

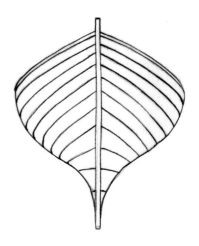

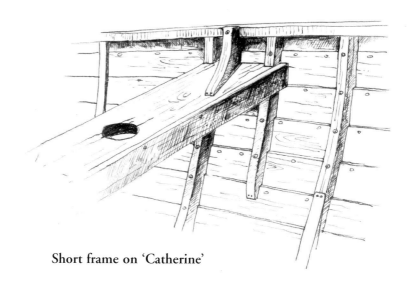

**Short frame on 'Catherine'**

On the Catherine the garboards are almost 'on end' on the sandstroke. Donald McFarlane's instruction to James Kelly when ordering a boat in 1910 was *'Cuir a cheud bord air oir'* (put the first plank on edge). It was the angle of sandstroke and garboard which decided whether a boat was 'fine' or 'flat'. The steeply angled sandstroke and garboard made the deeper-keeled 'sailing machine'. But the skiff needed to be more versatile than just a good sailing boat. The flatter section made for a better working boat in the local conditions of shallow bays, rocky beaches, and rough-water

coasts where oars were of more use than a sail.

A startling feature of the Kelly boat is the fact that it has no 'deadwood' in the bow, so close do the two garboards lie in to the keel and 'turn'. The Kelly boat, of course, was perfect for the Swan's Pool, as it was at anchor there and rarely beached. Boats for Port Charlotte or Partnahaven were made much shallower to be run up a beach.

**Deep midship frames and sandstroke 'Catherine'**

Hopkins traditionally built this 'flatter' boat.

On Islay, the sandstroke had extra stress placed on it, joined as it was to the keel with only two rows of nails, when coming into Loch Gruniart over its notorious sandbar.

*"Loaded with herring, coming in there on a dark night, through breakers, one touch and the keel was broken."*

But the sandstroke's great advantage was that it enabled the keel to be easily replaced. Jim describes the process at Loch Gruniart:

*"They had fellows there who would put a keel in for you in no time at all. It was common. They would do it with the boat sitting upright. They'd have raised her up on blocks and taken the keel out. They had the new keel measured and they sat her (the boat) on top, gave her a dunt (a blow) with a maul at both ends and she would drop on to the new keel."*

Other unusual features of the Kelly boat (or what Islay men wanted

Kelly to build into their boats!) included :

1 Two extra short frames on either shoulder between the long frames.

2 Most of the thirteen drontheim frames were equidistant apart but Kelly varied this according to perceived need for extra strength at different points. Spaces are narrower fore and aft but wider midships : from 16" at bow, to 18" at shoulder and 20" midships.

3 The midship frames are also made deeper in cross section than the others.

4 A beautifully fitted, tiny 'graving-piece' is also fitted for extra strength to the top 4 or 5ins. of both frames of the 'lifting' (loose) 5th beam.

5 Lastly, and perhaps Kelly's most distinctive and delicate detail was the traditional beading on the gunwale plank. Kelly added a line of beading along the outside gunwale as well and along the top of the inside of the 2nd last strake.... where it is seen, of course. This complements the same decoration on beams and wearing.

All this fine attention to detail has a Gaelic expression *Lurach*...'of tidy build' which beautifully sums up the functional and decorative craftsmanship of this forgotten builder.

'Catherine' is 25ft.6ins. x 7ft. x 2ft.9ins.

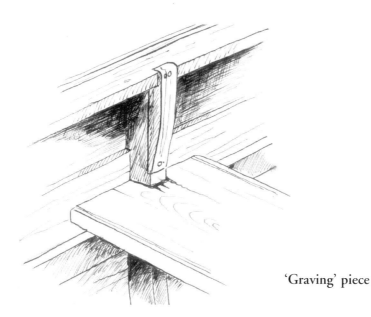

'Graving' piece

'Catherine' racing at Islay 1930

# FISHING

*"They were different men but there must have been a hell of a lot of suffering."*

Fishing began as early as February, but more usually March or April, with long-lining for plaice which came inshore to spawn on the great sandbanks.

In May boats were readied for the cod and saithe (coalfish) fishing. The 'saithe' or 'stenlock' were there all the year round and were fished at all stages of their growth. So intimate was the connection with this vital food source that there was a distinctive Gaelic name for each stage of its growth.

The tiny immature saithe was the *cuddag*, caught to this day by children but which in winter here long ago lay in the bays in great shoals and were harvested with fine - meshed seine nets. Boiled with a few nettles they made a nutritious soup.... bones and all!

The fully mature saithe was the *'ucsa'* or 'stenlock', a large heavy black coalfish, bigger than the cod; a fine fish and today, like so many other species, almost disappeared due to over-fishing.

In July and August the stenlock were fished for drying. They were then split, the bone taken out, salted, dried on the rocks in the open, and tied into bales. Loaded into skiffs they were sailed to Ballycastle for the Lammas Fair in late August. There they were bartered for all kinds of necessities. Little money changed hands. Skiffs came back with everything from pigs, goats, even horses, to goods for the kitchen and the winter larder.

When the summer sun went down the saithe came to the surface and were fished with long bamboo poles (much like the Portuguese tunny fishermen!), a short line and a single hook tied on a horsehair 'snood'. The hook was a 'fly' tied with the feathers milked from the tail feathers of a black-backed gull.

With the loose beam lifted and set across the aft gunwale one or two men fished up to 6 rods, 'two under your arse and one with tip under'.

Two men rowed slowly and the fish rose in great numbers to the fly, so thick and fast there was little time for anything except hook, lift, board, and cast again. Great shoals of mackeral in June or July were caught the same way. Such an abundance of fish almost unknown and unremembered today!

## LONG LINES
## *(Lín mbóra)*

Plaice (or flounder) were taken on the long lines which were cotton, preserved by soaking with the traditional Catticue. A line consisted of 12 'bolts' and a bolt contained 25 hooks. The hook was at the end of a 'snood' - half cotton or hemp line and half horsehair. The horsehair snood consisted of several hairs from a horse's tail or mane twisted with a spinning pot-lid. (Hair from the mare's tail was weaker and had to be twisted back on itself again to be as strong as that of the stallion!) Hooks were baited with lugworm.

The farthest off the skiffs fished was at the 'middle bank' about 8 miles west of the 'Oa' (Islay's

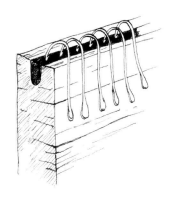

*line, pushed it through the skin or flesh and out again!"*

A spit of tobacco sealed the cut or ashore a bunch of cobwebs stenched the wound. Herbs dug from a garden or ditch prevented infection and healed wounds before antibiotics.

After the season lines were washed in a fresh-water burn for a day to remove the corrosive salt. Rust and dried bait was scraped from the old steel hooks and the now bright sharp tips were placed in rows in the groove of old 'tongue and groove' floorboard pieces with the groove now filled with wax. This kept the hooks dry and sharp in the damp winter days before stainless steel.

## THE "DIVIDE" *(An Roinn)*

Ashore, the catch had to be divided as evenly as possible and a simple

southernmost headland ) in terrible tide races which meant they could only be fished at slack water and in neap tides.

Lines were also used for haddock fishing and these were shot when the sun went down and hauled almost immediately, when the first star appeared in the sky.

Shooting a long-line was a skilful business and even the most careful could get a hook in finger or hand.

*"If a hook went in it stayed in until lanced by the doctor at home. Old men lanced it themselves with a tobacco knife, or cut it from the*

**The 'Divide', Port Charlotte c.1902**

method was devised. *"If there were three men, three heaps of fish were made. One man turned his back and looked away. One of the other crewmen pointed to one heap of fish and said 'Who's taking that.' The man with this back turned could name someone to take it. So it was done fairly with each pile."*

## RACING

*"Off the wind, nothing, absolutely nothing could look at an Irish Skiff."*

There was always great pleasure in racing here with the skiffs. The last races here, as in Ireland were in the 1950s when 10 - 12 skiffs took part.

At these races the great standing lugs were introduced, mostly taking the place of the usual two sprit sails which nevertheless still competed with them. The lugsail was mounted with two jibs which were set on a bowsprit mounted on a 'saddle' across the forward gunwales.... a bowsprit which was slotted over the long stem-head of the skiff rather than at its side. The outer jib was always larger for off-the-wind work

and both were rarely used together. Working to windward the smaller was used to get the boat up but on a reach the small jib came down and the big jib was set flying to maximum effect.

Any rig, in fact, was acceptable for these races. Some skiffs even had washboards but false keels were not allowed.

Handicaps were determined solely by waterline length. In a race any ballast started with had to be finished with. None could be jettisoned to lighten the boat on a homeward

run. Nor could an oar be used to come about!

The lug was called the 'Big Rig'. Only in very strong conditions could the spritsail compete with the lug and it made for exciting and often dangerous racing. But the men delighted in the speed and danger and pushed the boats to the limit for a day's sport.

The best sails were kept for racing. Anything might do for fishing (even flour bags had been used in the 40s, ripped out, cut, ropes and seams sewn on and all catticued a dark red!). But soft 'Egyptian' cotton was best and preferably roped with Italian hemp.

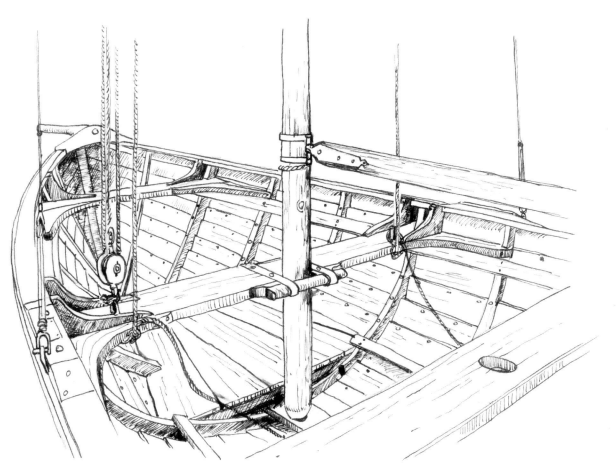

The 'Kathleen' rigged for a lug-sail 1996

Manila would shrink when wet, and lengthen when dry, often ruining the set of the sail. Latterly the leading edge of the lug-sail was of wire, keeping the sail edge as tight and straight to the wind as possible. The light racing sails were left white, unlike the working sails. The bottom of the racing skiff was often polished smooth with 'black lead'(used for polishing the old iron kitchen ranges) to give extra speed.

## DISASTERS

*"On the whole they were good safe boats and in good hands."*

Losses were inevitable with open boats on such a wild coast but they were not many. Long ago an Irish family coming from Ireland were lost out of a skiff in Stremnish Bay. To this day the reef they hit is called *"Bodha na hEireannach"*... the Irish reef.

Before the turn of the century it was remembered that a skiff, hit by a squall ran on to a reef, filled and went over. It was unfortunately carrying firebars from the boiler of a steamer as ballast instead of the

Jim McFarlane and 'Kathleen' sailing at Islay 1997

traditional round stones. The firebars jammed on the beams as she capsized and the boat sank.

## THE END

*"How they managed there with rowing boats I'll never know. God only knows."*

When engines appeared they were quickly adopted by the skiff owners. They had no love for the hardships of sail and oar!

*"There was such hardship with sails and oars, many's a cussing and suffering I heard at one of those little headlands, men trying to get round in a breeze of wind. They would rather tack for a mile than row a hundred yards.... You couldn't get an engine into the boat fast enough!"*

But the engines proved too much for the light skiffs. Conversion began after the last war but only a few lasted to the 60s. None of the engines was a success. Here too they did terrible damage to the light skiffs, bursting the planks forward, or the frames. They shook them

apart, literally, often starting at the sandstroke. *"They were made to rise over everything, not be driven down by a propeller."*

The last skiffs came to Islay about 1925 - 35 and when they were worn out like the men who knew how to sail them, they quietly disappeared here as on the Irish coast. One remained in the beach at Port Ellen, latterly ferrying cattle to Texa island but later left to rot. Jim McFarlane

rescued the old 'Catherine' at almost her last breath. She was used as the model for the new skiff 'Kathleen' built in 1996. Both lay beside each other at the end of the Bay in Port Ellen. 'Catherine' has now returned to the new museum in Portrush … perhaps not quite the end after all.

# DISASTERS

*"Them days we knowed nothin and feared nothin".*

(Henry Canning)

There are no great losses of boats in living memory but local folk memory, old newspaper reports, and lighthouse records give us a small insight into the perilous and often tragic world of open-boat sailing and fishing. Men still talk about 'Black Saturday' 1772. The entire fleet from Lough Foyle was lost near the 'Tuns' bank when 13 boats and upwards of 30 men were lost fishing hand lines. One survivor was washed ashore clinging to an oar. 66 widows were left.

*"A freak gale came out of nothing and blew them all to hell - only a cripple, a disabled man was saved."*

(Bob Cavanagh)

Hugh McCann and Bob Cavanagh of Strove both had stories of the terrible return of drowned men.

*"One of the Smiths of the Green Hill was lost and his father dreamed he'd come in over there at Port Cill. He was that sure he did go round, sure enough, he got the son.*

*"One Campbell man was drowned at lines in the dark. He was lost. A few days after, a child asleep in a cage bed awoke to see him sitting at the fire, fully rigged in his oilskins. This happened a couple of nights and then the father saw him. 'What in the name of God do you want?' He said, 'My body will rise at the stern of McCann's boat.' And one day in daylight after they'd boarded the line, the body came up. They wrapped it in a jib and towed it after the boat. You see a body in the water for a long time is a terrible sight."*

Barney McKenna relates a near disaster when a crew were caught by a gale long-lining out between Inishtrahull and Malin Head. They stayed too long at the lines and had to run before the gale. They couldn't get into Inishtrahull and were blown away to Rathlin. Their drontheim was almost completely filled with water. In panic one crewman threw out their tin baler and the desperate men then bailed with their boots! Eventually they reached Church Bay in Rathlin 40 miles away. From there they were brought home by a Fleetwood Trawler. At Glengad, in the meantime, after two days they had been given up for dead and had been waked!

The local blacksmith who heard of their return as he was shoeing a horse had this comment: *"Every man should get a slat mara and lay into them boys"....* presumably for their carelessness in getting caught in a storm when they shouldn't have. No sympathy in Glengad for careless boatmen in those days!

The trawler which brought the men home took the drontheim back on her deck as well. Ironically, when putting it back in the water in Glengad they put a hook in the side of it causing it to capsize and sink!

FROM THE LIGHTKEEPERS
JOURNAL OF INISHOWEN
WEST LIGHTHOUSE
JANUARY 2nd, 1877

"A similar accident occurred off Glengad on this date. During a sudden squall the boats belonging to that port, that were out fishing, were blown out to sea. One boat and crew were swamped and 7 men drowned. Two boats made the Scotch coast in safety and a third drifted to Rathlin island. Two of the crew of the latter were dead on reaching that island...."

January 15th 1878: "At 4 p.m. as a boat was returning from Moville, the crew having sold their fish and on entering a small boat harbour this side of Greencastle struck on a rock and upset. One man was drowned. Drink is said to be the cause of the disaster".

February 15th 1878: "This evening a melancholy accident occurred at the Warren Port Lighthouse resulting in the loss of two lives. Two fishermen named Clark and Doherty had been in Moville selling fish with others and were on their way home when the boat capsized. Three of the crew were saved by a boat that put off from the shore".

May 7th 1883: "At 2.30 p.m. the wind blowing NE, a fleet of fishing yawls off the Head (Inishowen Head) was overtaken by a sudden storm of wind and while in the act of endeavouring to make the harbour, one of the boats with a crew of four mean was upset. The men managed to cling to the boat until rescued by a comrade yawl. But sad to relate, one of the other yawls with a crew of four men was lost. The boat was picked up next morning in the South Channel bottom aloft".

January 31st 1891 : "On this morning at 6 o'clock during a strong gale, a small fishing boat with five men belonging to Tremone Bay went out to haul lines and was blown off the land. She was seen about 2 miles east off Inishowen Head. At 12 noon, a fishing boat belonging to Shrove with 8 men went out to her assistance and towed her ashore, her crew being exhausted. The life-boat also went off but the Shrove boat had her picked up first".

November 23rd 1889 : "During a strong gale from the east, a fishing yawl belonging to Shrove, with five men of a crew, was capsized, abreast of the West Lighthouse about 11 a.m. Three of her crew were drowned and two saved by the Pilot Boat who went off to their assistance".

From the "LONDONDERRY STANDARD" 28th January 1831

## MELANCHOLY OCCURRENCE WITH LOSS OF LIVES

It seldom has fallen to our lot to record a more distressing occurrence than the following :

On Monday last, the 24th instant, about twenty fishing boats, mostly from Shrove, near Ennishowen Head, Greencastle, Whitebay, etc. proceeded to the Isle Bank, about ten miles distant from Lough Foyle. The morning was fine, wind S.W. However, about one o'clock, the horizon all at once became clouded, and a most dreadful gale of wind came on from the N.N.E.

On the first appearance of danger a number of these boats cut away from their lines, and made for the land, whilst others waited to lift their lines, and, dreadful to relate, five boats' crews, consisting of twenty-one men, met a watery grave, leaving behind them seventy-three helpless children. The arrival of the first boats' crew at Greencastle brought the lamentable intelligence that they had seen several boats capsize. Immediately the families of the missing and others, in a distracted state, proceeded to Shrove-head, a distance of two miles, and could perceive some of the boats dashed upon the"Tuns", and even the persons in them clapping their hands in agony and despair. One young man swam to the shore, but was dashed to pieces on a rock in sight of many persons, who could render him no assistance. Such a scene has not been witnessed there since what was termed the "Black Saturday", about fifty-eight years ago.The cries of the wives, children, and relations were most heartrending. We have heard that a boat at Malin, with seven men on board, has also been lost.

No record has been yet found of what happened on 'Black Saturday' but it is still part of the folk memory of Inishowen. The following appeared again in the Londonderry Standard 1831.

"There was a rumour here on last Thursday of another calamity off Ennishowen head, involving a loss of lives nearly as great as that which occurred some weeks before. It was that eighteen fishermen had perished in a gale on Thursday week. This rumour has proved but too well founded, though not to the extent at first apprehended by the distracted relatives of these persons. Five men have lost their lives - the others were picked up by the schooner Prince Coburg, of Kirkwall. She fortunately described their perilous situation and with great difficulty saved the lives of four boats' crews consisting of fourteen men, with the exception of one who was drowned in trying to get from the boat to the schooner. The master treated them with humanity, and landed them safely at Ballina, where they arrived here on Wednesday last. In addition to Eneas McDonnell who was lost as above stated, one boats' crew was wholly lost, consisting of Hugh O'Donnell, Edward McDavitt, Daniel McCarran and James Doherty. We have no doubt that the families of these ill-fated men will be relieved from the subscriptions which have been raised for those of the former sufferers."

## RATHLIN

The folklore collector Michael J. Murphy talked to a woman in Rathlin in the 1940s whose grandmother had told her of two Rathlin boats and their crews lost on a trip to Islay.

*"They were goin' with barley. It brought a good price that time from a distillery down there. It was around Christmas time and it had come on sleet and snow and wind and they went. Some of them were got off Derry after, and some of them there was never a bit of word of."*

In a sailing boat the worst mistake a man can make is to tie the sheet of the mainsail.

*"John Anderson was going to Ballycastle. Two boats were going to an election. He was the helmsman and he tied the sheet... The boat hit a squall and was upset. He was the only one was lost."*

(Loughie McQuilkin)

Loughie's uncle was drowned in 1911 coming back form Ballycastle.

*"He stood up on a beam to peak the sail. The rope broke and he went right over the gunwale. Before they got the boat about he had disappeared. They had been over for a coffin for a man who had died. It wasn't even his boat. He'd just made up a crew.... They never got his body. There had been reports that it came ashore somewhere on the Ayrshire coast. They said it might have been him by the socks he was wearing."*

**The Last Greencastle Fishing Drontheim c. 1975**

**Drontheims at Moville Regatta c.1936**
With borrowed yacht-rigs, washboards and bow-sprit saddles (Courtesy Norris Kane)

# CONCLUSION

*A beautiful thing.......*

*One is loathe to refer to the drontheim as a beautiful thing. Such a term is not common in the harsh realities of fishing. A boat's first and last purpose was that of a tool for the the men making a living on the open sea where romantic notions would have been out of place.*

*However, there is undoubtedly an affection among fishermen for their own boats, for their graceful lines, for the skill of its builder, for its sailing or handling qualities, for the fine sight it may make at a summer regatta or rushing before a good breeze of wind. Why else would the Viking chieftains have had their boats buried with them if there was not such an affection?*

*There used to be an idea that if a construction followed impeccably the laws of its own necessity, it would automatically become beautiful. This is true of a sailing boat but untrue of a fork- lift truck. Perhaps one can say that if a man-made object has to contend with the elements and as the drontheim or Viking gallery contended with the Atlantic swells then some kind of resolute economy that we call beauty may be the result. In this regard the drontheim was very beautiful indeed.*

# APPENDIX 1

Technical Description of the Greencastle Yawl or Drontheim

by Kevin McLaverty B.Sc. C.Eng. M.R.I.N.A.

B.I.M. National Fishery Training Centre, Greencastle, Co. Donegal.

This technical description of the Greencastle Yawl or Drontheim is based on a study of the 26 foot yawl housed at the National Fishery Training College, Greencastle, Co. Donegal, for the Ulster Folk and Transport Museum. The description is complimented where necessary, by a study of the few remaining derelict boats in the district and old photographs.

The description, and sketches, here are intended to enable a replica of a typical drontheim to be built at some future date.

(Kevin McLaverty Nov. 1991)

## INTRODUCTION

A distinctive, traditional boat type found in a particular coastal area such as the Scottish Zulu, the Yorkshire Coble, the Galway Hooker or the Falmouth Quay Punt is essentially the final product of three influences :

(i) Ancestry (ii) Purpose and (iii) Working conditions, including the socio/economic background.

(i) The Drontheim's ancestry can be traced directly to Norway.

(ii) The boat's purpose was line fishing, drift netting and the transport of goods and animals to Rathlin Island and the various islands off County Donegal.

(iii) The boat's working conditions were the tide-riven coastal water and narrow stony beaches off North Donegal and Antrim.In these areas, fishing alone was insufficient to support the community, so this was supplemented with farming. The land was poor and fishing harbours non-existent, so the communities lived a life of unremitting hardship and isolation. The Drontheim was unique, being devoid of any concession to the non-essential in dimensions, building materials or fittings.

That the development of the Drontheim was fully crystallised and complete can be established by the study of old photographs and remaining examples of existing boats. All Drontheims were virtually identical in size, form and method of construction, the smaller 20- 22ft. and the larger 26- 28ft.

The exceptional features of Drontheim form and construction are reviewed below, together with some attempt at assigning the influences giving rise to these features.

## GENERAL HULL FORM AND CONSTRUCTION :

The drontheim could be technically described as a double-ended clinker built open boat, basically twenty six feet long, with a six and a half to seven foot beam and a moulded depth of two and a half feet, propelled by either oars or sails.The planking was of larch or deal and the internal framing was sawn oak.

A double-ended vessel is basically a boat where the stern is pointed and has the same construction as the bow. This type of construction is inherently Scandinavian. A vessel with this feature allows a greatly varying load to be carried in the boat, without destroying the streamline form aft. This was important in the Drontheim when the power available was limited to oars. It also had advantages when a vessel had to be beached, perhaps through surf, allowing the vessel to approach the shore bow first. The double-ended hull form also circumvented the weaknesses inherent in the "edges" of transom-stern construction and was much better suited to the working of drift nets and fishing lines off the sides of the boat.

The hull lines of the drontheim were extremely well-balanced, being almost symmetrical about the midship section. The waterlines and sections forward and aft were hollow and supremely fine. The line of the gunwale was reasonably full, giving good reserve buoyancy above the water. The stem and stern lines were straight, only the stem showing a slight rake. The sheet was moderately sprung.

The midship section showed a reverse curve in the garboards and the flare of the topsides, being carried all the way up to the sheer, gave a good beam at the gunwale with a narrower beam at the waterline. The midship section looked very Scandinavian indeed, but the lack of overhangs and the moderate sheer were less so.

In general, the fine lines indicated a boat that should be easily rowed, yet a good load carrier for her size. The flare and sheer ensured an able, dry seaboat, while the deep keel indicated a boat that must have sailed well with a moderate, close-winded sail plan of moderate weight.

The drontheim was clinker built, again proclaiming her Scandinavian origins. In clinker boatbuilding, the shell planking is assembled first and each plank overlaps the one below and is close rivetted to it throughout its entire length. The clinker method allows a rigid watertight shell to be completed with much thinner planks than carvel building, where the plank edges have to carry caulking. Drontheim planking was

just over ⅜in. thick, whereas the equivalent in carvel building would be one inch thick. The saving in weight and materials can be imagined.

The size of the drontheim was dictated by the environment where the boats worked. There were virtually no fishing harbours on the north coast of Ireland, so the boats had to be kept ashore above the high water mark when not in use; the water being too exposed to leave the boats afloat. Unlike the west of Ireland where there are sandy beaches and the tidal range is large, where the highly portable curragh reigns supreme, the north coast beaches are mostly shingle and the tidal range is such that the distance between low water and high water is much less. The drontheim was essentially the largest vessel that could be manhandled out of the water by her crew, without special equipment. The crew size, usually four men, was dictated by the nature of the fishing communities which were small and isolated. Four men representing the minimum number for balanced rowing, with one man steering. The beam of the drontheim

was dictated by the requirements for rowing, recognising that eighteen foot oars are about the largest feasible length for one man to manage and that the usual ratio of inboard to outboard length was maintained. The depth of the drontheim was also dictated by the rowing requirements. If the depth were increased, the freeboard (the height of the boat out of the water) would also be increased. If this were the case, the looms of the oars would have been too high in the boat for satisfactory pulling.

## THE KEEL AND CENTRE-LINE STRUCTURE:

The keel of the drontheim was comparatively small in cross section and was also unusually deep and thin in section. A boatbuilder would describe it as light in scantling with a large moulded depth and small siding. Again, this showed a Scandinavian influence. There was a strong inference, from the keel and associated construction, that the keel was considered as a readily replaceable item rather than the fundamental 'backbone' of Central

European construction. This was certainly reasonable for a boat which was beached on stony shores, twice in a day's work.

The stern and sternposts, i.e. the continuation of the keel up the line of the bow the stern, were also of small siding and were joined to the keel with vertical scarphs (tapered joints). This was uniquely Scandinavian as the thin siding was insufficient to accommodate vertical bolts or drifts in the more usual horizontal scarphs. With this construction, it was impossible to fit stopwaters and the scarphs were usually sealed with Archangel tar.

### The Sandstroke

The keel was also too thin to accommodate a rabbet for the hull planking and a hog was not fitted. (The rabbet is a right-angled groove cut along each side of the stem and stern post sides to accommodate the ends of the planks. The planks thus finish flush with the sides of the posts, yet maintain their full thickness). Use was made of a 'sandstroke' between the garboard proper and the keel (the garboard is normally the lowest or first plank next to the keel). The sandstroke was unique to Northern Irish boatbuilding and was a variant of the hewn garboards to be seen to this day in traditional boatbuilding in Norway.

Sandstrokes were narrow planks fitted to each side of the keel running the entire length of the keel. They were bevelled on the edges which face onto the keel. The bevel of the sandstrokes amidships were cut to match the rise of floor amidships and the bevels tapered to the vertical at bow and stern. As well as the varying bevel, the width of the sandstrokes tapered to nothing at bow and stern and they were fastened to each side of the keel with galvanised boat nails throughout their length. This fashioning of sandstrokes was one of these inherently traditional skills, being a subtle combination of springing, setting and bevelling of the plank, defying any rigorous geometrical approach to this layout. The elegant traditional skill of fashioning sandstrokes must, unfortunately, die with the last boat-builders capable of making them.

Similar to the keel, the stem and stern post were also too small in siding to accommodate the usual planking rabbet. In Drontheim construction, the plank ends were very accurately bevelled and nailed to the sides of the stem and stern post. This bevelling of the plank ends is seen in Norwegian wooden boat-building from the Gokstad ship to the present day. This construction is not seen in Central Europe where the stem and stern post rabbet is typical, backed perhaps with an apron.

An apron was fitted on the inside face of both stem and stern posts to increase the landing area of the plank ends. Unlike the modern sternpost, built to accommodate a propeller, the traditional Donegal Drontheim stern post was rounded at the base and faired into the line of the keel. With the rudder un-shipped, this allowed the boat to be turned round more easily on the beach. The keel bottom was slightly rockened for the same reason. This rounded stern post is also in the Scandinavian tradition.

## PLANKING

The planking of the Drontheim was ⁹⁄₁₆" thick larch or deal laid clinker or lapstrake as already explained. The lands were rivetted with copper nails and rooves pitched 6".

In clinker boat-building, where the line of the plank laps or 'lands' are there for all to see, the fairness of the lands and the eye-sweet tapering of the planks denotes the work of a master craftsman as distinct from the merely adequate. Recognising this, an unusual tradition becomes apparent on the study of Drontheim planking. The first, or lowest, three or four planks on each side were noticeably wider than the remainder of the planks. Also the usual taper towards bow and stern was not obvious; the reverse being apparent as the planks appeared to gain in width at the stem and stern posts; this used to be termed 'fishtailing' in boat-building parlance.

Why this should be so in drontheim is difficult to explain, though the lack of taper can again be found in Norway. It may be a product of the unusually fine lines in the ends of the Drontheim, coupled with a desire to economise on planking materials.

It should be noted here that the drontheim was traditionally planked in two phases. The bottom was planked (the old builders used the term 'spread') for three or four planks each side. Planking was then halted while the bottom members of the framing were installed. The builders temporary building moulds or 'shadows' were then fitted and faired up to the sheer line with battens. The planking was then continued up to the sheer and then the remainder of the framing installed.

It could be inferred from this that perhaps the drontheim evolved from the basic Norwegian fjord boat, which had only three or four wide planks, to a somewhat larger boat, with built-up topsides to accommodate the rougher water off the North Irish Coast.

Nimmo Report 1822. St. John's Point to Bangor. *"Norway Yawls,*

*heightened one strake and rowed by 4 men"*

## FRAMING

The framing of the Drontheim consisted of sawn oak, transverse frames of elegantly light scantlings, relatively widely-spaced: typically 20" amidships and 24" at the ends. Traditionally, the frames were close-fitted and faced onto the planks throughout the whole width of each plank. The accuracy of fit over the differing bevels of each plank, as done by master builders such as McDonalds of Moville, was a delight to see. This close fitting contributed greatly to the durability of a boat which received rough treatment grounding on the beach (this close fitting is also to be seen on Yorkshire Cobles which are also efficient beach boats).

Unusually, the frames were not fastened to the keel, there usually being a limber hole in the base of the frame which straddled the keel top and both sandstrokes. This allowed a degree of flexibility in the bottom of a vessel expected to ground heavily on beaches. It also allowed easy

replacement of the keel structure. It should be recognised that the siding of the keel was insufficient to carry fastenings in any event.

Drontheims were built in the days when oak with swept grain was available (the grain of the wood followed the curve of the frame). This enabled the frames to be built in three parts or 'futtocks'. The bottom futtock straddled the keel and the two side futtocks carried the frame up to each gunwale. In older boats, the side futtocks were scarphed to the bottom futtock just below the turn of the bilge. This unusual scarph on the inside face of the frame is again peculiarly Scandinavian and has virtually died out of boat-building now. In later boats, the futtocks were lapped together; this is more common and is found, for instance, in the construction of Galway Hookers.

The frame station next to the stem and next to the stern post was filled with a light oak bent timber instead of a frame. This was through-rivetted in the same way as steamed timbers in conventional clinker building. In the case of the fine-

Finishing a swept-grain timber.
Brian McDonald 1996

linked drontheim, this timber was probably bent in cold. The space to swing a rivetting hammer here must have been very limited indeed!

## GUNWALES

The sheer stringers, or gunwales, of the drontheim were of substantial construction. They were made of larch or deal and fitted inside the planking level with the sheer and run over the tops of the frames. Unusually, the gunwales were not bent but sawn to shape, having a siding of $2\frac{1}{2}$" amidships tapering to 1" at the bow and stern. The gunwales also tapered in moulding from $1\frac{1}{4}$" amidships to 1" at the bow and stern. Being sawn, the gunwales were fitted in three pieces per side. The pieces were scarphed, the scarph faces being vertical. The scarphs were rather short compared with modern practice, but arranged so that they were reinforced by the thwart hanging knees.

The gunwale carried the $1\frac{1}{4}$ diameter tapered holes for the oar thole-pins without any reinforcement other than short replaceable oak protecting pads in way of each pair of thole pins, locally called 'rowths'.

The usual breasthooks, generally of oak or elm with swept grain, were fitted fore and aft. An elegant featured to be noted here is that the aprons were carried up the inside face of the stem and stern posts above the line of the sheer to finish flush with the head of each post. The aprons were thus stiffened by the gunwale ends and the breasthooks. The top ends of the aprons were neatly faired with the post sides and top. A 1" timber half-round capping strip was fitted on the outside of the planking at the sheer line.

## THWARTS

The thwarts, usually termed 'seats' by the layman and known locally as 'beams' were substantial, being 9" x 2" larch. There were six of them in all, lightly checked into a light continuous stringer, or riser, locally termed the 'wearing' or 'bearer'. The ends of all the thwarts except one, were reinforced with $1\frac{1}{4}$" thick, oak, double hanging knees, each checked $\frac{1}{4}$" into the gunwale timber. The knees were tapered out along the thwarts with long elegantly shaped arms. A strong construction was necessary here because the thwarts carried the loads of masts without the support of any standing rigging. It is interesting that in some cases no lodging knees were fitted to any thwart. The light checking of the hanging knees into the gunwale members proved sufficient for the stresses of sailing and manhandling out of the water.

The fourth thwart from forward was removable and dropped into place in a notch on the riser. The thwart itself was also notched to fit over the adjacent frame. When in place, the thwart was thus held fixed fore and aft and athwartships. This traditional, removable, thwart appears to have been fitted to open up the waist of the boat for cargo, such as sheep being carried to and from the islands, and to accommodate the bulk of drift nets used for salmon or herring fishing.

The two forward thwarts carried a forged iron mast gate in later examples. In the older boats, a traditional system, using a wedge, was fitted. Both mast gate systems allowed the masts to be stepped quickly from inside the boat. The third thwart from forward carried a conventional mast hole through the middle.

## ROWING ARRANGEMENTS

As already mentioned, pairs of rowing pins could be slipped through oak reinforcing pads or 'rowths' on the gunwales. Sets of pins were fitted on both sides of the boat to accommodate oarsmen on the second, third, fourth and fifth thwarts from forward. The thwarts in the ends of the boat were generally too high and short to permit rowing.

The standard oars were made of clear pine and measured eighteen feet in length. Typically, the blades were 4" x 1",.... elliptical in section at the tips. The blades tapered over approximately seven feet to a circular section 2½" at the neck. The section then faired into a 3" x 3" square section loom to within 14" of the pulling end, where it again tapered to a round section about 2" in diameter. The corners of the square loom were slightly radiused.

Oar leathers were not fitted; but oars were 'roped'. Where the square-sectioned loom of a 'box' oar passed between the rowing pins, replaceable wooden pads were nailed on three sides to take the inevitable wear. These pads extended over 24" or so and were some ⅜" thick. Few stretchers or foot bars were fitted; apparently a foot planted on the

edge of the next thwart aft had to suffice when rowing!

## SAILING GEAR

The sailing gear was an outstanding compromise of simplicity and efficiency, being easily stepped and un-stepped in the boat as the demands of weather, rowing and fishing required. The rig allowed an excellent spread of sail to be set with the minimum of spars and rigging. It was obviously important that the sailing gear should take up as little room as possible when not in use.

It would appear that when sailing to the local grounds and back, a single mast was stepped at the second thwart from forward. This mast carried a sprit sail permanently bent to the mast along the luff, and set loose footed. A foresail was set flying from a single block at the masthead with a halyard belayed on the windward side of the thwart supporting the mast. The foresail tack was secured at a hole through the stem-head.

**G. Divers 24ft boat under restoration Ballybrack 1997**

When racing under the 'fishing rig', a second mast carrying an identical sprit sail could be stepped through the third thwart from forward. When this was done, the original mast was stepped at the first thwart from forward to preserve the balance of the rig.

When sailing under the two-masted rig, the foresail could also be set from the forward mast. In this instance, the foresail was tacked down to a bowsprit, locally termed a 'jib stick', which extended some 6 feet over the bow. The bowsprit was either set without fittings, being seized to the side of the fore-mast and the stem-head with a lashing, or mounted on a home-made 'saddle' fitted across the gunwales.

All the sheets were single lengths of rope tied to the clew of each sail and the sheets were transferred across the boat when tacking. There were no foresail sheet fairleads, the sheets being passed round a pin on the underside of the gunwale or under the 'wearing' aft of a suitable frame. The sheet loads of the sprit sails must have been considerable and these sheets were passed under the fifth and sixth thwarts and round special pins projecting aft from below each thwart at their outboard ends.

All the spars were grown sticks, the mast being straight tapered from heel to head, (there were no trucks or head sheaves fitted). The heels of the masts were pointed bluntly, so that the masts could be stepped without any alignment fore and aft. Both ends of the sprit were tapered bluntly to accommodate the beckits in the head of the sail and the beckit on the mast above the tack of the sail.

The sails were made of cotton or flax canvas and 'barked' i.e. they were tanned along with the nets using oak bark. This acted as a preservative. Unusually, the sails were roped all round and no noticeable roach was cut on any edge. The cloths of the sails followed the line of the leach which was the old, vertical seaming system. No false seams or extensive tabling were incorporated in the sails. The sails were obviously made locally, entirely by hand.

The rudder, the other essential fitting for sailing, was simple but its fittings were well developed for the awkward operation of shipping and un-shipping a rudder in a seaway. All the rudder hangings were from forgings obviously made by a local blacksmith. The lower rudder pintle was exceptionally long and curved to match the line of the sternpost. This engaged in a gudgeon fitted to the lower part of the sternpost. The upper gudgeon was fitted to the rudder, instead of its usual position on the boat, and this was engaged by a unique dropping bolt system fitted across a notch in the upper part of the sternpost. At sea, this allowed the rudder to be shipped by engaging the lower pintle, where its length made this easy, then aligning the rudder roughly and dropping the captive bolt through the upper gudgeon on the rudder.

The rudder was operated with a relatively short straight tiller engaging in a mortise in the rudder head. The rudder head was fitted with conventional side cheeks.

There were traditionally two mast steps fitted to accommodate the three possible mast positions. These were made of oak, the forward step, below the first thwart, carried a single hole for the heel of the mast. The after step sometimes extended below both the second and third thwarts and carried two holes. Unusually, the holes in the steps were round and were tapered to accommodate the heels of the masts. As mentioned, this permitted the masts to be stepped without the trouble of aligning the more usual mortise and tenon arrangement. The loads on the steps must have been considerable and they were lightly checked into the frames to lock them athwartships.

## FITTINGS

Drontheims were unique in their lack of any sophisticated metal fittings, these being confined to the rudder fittings, as already described, and a keel band. In some later boats, two forged, hinged, mast gates were fitted. There was literally not so much as a ring bolt, cleat or chainplate to be seen anywhere!

The drainage bung, locally called the 'duck' or 'spile', was an important fixture as, once beached, it was necessary to drain the boat of bilge water and remove the ballast before she could be hauled above the high water mark. Getting to the bung of a boat loaded with nets, fish and bilge water could be difficult. This was elegantly accomplished in the Drontheim. The duck consisted of a slowly tapered staff a foot or more in length. This engaged in a slowly tapered hole, bored in the top edge of the keel, inside the boat, right aft. The tapered hole in the top edge of the keel did not go all the way through the depth of the keel but connected with another hold bored horizontally through the keel, just below the planking. The duck was thus easily accessible and at the lowest point of a boat which had landed bows first on a shelving beach. The draining of the boat was unobstructed with sand or shingle as it took place from the sides of the keel rather than the bottom.

## PAINTING

The drontheim was first coated with linseed oil - up to five coats - and the inside liberally painted with Stockholm or Archangel tar. Unlike coal tar, Stockholm tar hardens with a dry outer skin. The centre of the thwarts and the spars were generally left unpainted, perhaps for better friction.

The outside of the drontheim planking and the gunwale timbers were usually primed with red lead paint and then finished with coats of white lead paint. In some cases, the sheer planks were painted a contrasting colour, usually light blue or green. All the boats once owned by one agent in Greencastle were painted completely green!

## CONCLUSION

When the last pulling and sailing Drontheims were built in the 1950s, they represented the outcome of centuries of relatively isolated development in the face of extremely limited local material and manpower resources. It can be appreciated that the true beauty of the Drontheim lay in the elegantly concise answer she presented to the demands made upon her, rather than any sophistication of rig or fittings.

Bernard Baris restored 1952 24ft. Drontheim Moville 1996

The 1999 Drontheim "James Kelly"

# GLOSSARY

**AFT** The rear or stern part of a boat

**ARCHANGEL TAR** A thick bituminous tar once imported from the port of Archangel in northern Russia

**BEAM** The width of a ship from side to side, or the thwarts or seats in a boat which are fixed from side to side.

**BLOCK** A pulley wheel with a wood exterior used in various ways in the boat's rigging.

**BLUESTONE** Copper-sulphate which is used as a spray against potato-blight.

**BOOM** A long pole extending from the mast towards or over the stern of a boat and which stretches the bottom edge (or 'foot') of the sail.

**BOWSPRIT** A pole extending forward from the bow of a boat, the end of which holds the tack of the jib or first sail.

**CARVEL** A boat type in which the hull planks are flush laid edge to edge and the seams caulked giving a smooth hull appearance.

**A 'CLEAN' BOAT** One which takes in little water over her bows in a heavy sea.

**DIPPING-LUG** An asymmetrical square-sail which has to be lowered and carried round the mast when turning the boat on to a different tack

**DOUBLE BANKED** Two men sitting side by side at the same oar.

**DULSE** An edible seaweed.

**FRAMES** The internal oak 'ribs' of a boat, also called 'timbers', the planks being nailed or rivetted on to them from outside.

**FREEBOARD** The height of the side of the vessel above the waterline.

**GAFF-RIGGED** A four sided main-sail with a spar along its upper edge projecting out and above the mast to increase the sail's height and volume.

**GARBOARD** The strake next to the sandstroke or keel.

**GUNWALE** The upper edge of a boat's side.

**HALLIARD** A rope used for hoisting a sail.

**HOOD-END** That part of a strake where it is joined to the stem or stern-post.

**JIB HALLIARD** The line on which the head of the jib is hauled to the top of the mast.

**KNEE** Crooked or L shaped pieces of timber (usually oak)which connect the beams of a boat with its sides and gunwale

**LANDS** The overlaps of clinker planks.

**LOOM** The shaft part of an oar above the blade.

**MOULD** Transverse wooden patterns which determine the hull shape at different points, along the length of the boat. Sometimes called 'Shadows'

**PLANK** A shaped board forming the shell of the hull

**QUARTERS** The stern or after parts of a boat each side of the centre line i.e. the starboard quarter and port quarter.

**RABBET** A grove cut on the stem and sternpost to take the ends of the planking.

**ROACH** A curve worked in the edge of a sail to give it extra fullness.

**ROOVED** The plank lands fastened with copper rivets.

**RUNNING END** This is the free end of a rope as distinct from the 'standing part' which is fixed to something.

**SCARP** A method of joining planks end to end by tapering their end faces and overlapping one on the other.

**'SET FLYING'** The sail is supported at each corner only.

**SHEER** The curve of the line of the gunwale or upper edge between bow and stern.

**SHEERSTRAKE** The top strake of an open boat.

**SHEET** A rope attached to the aft corner of a sail which controls the angle of the sail to the wind.

**'SLAT MARA'** A Gaelic word for the rod-like end of a common sea weed.

**STAY** A supporting rope or wire running from the masthead forward to the stem-head or down to the side of the boat.

**STEM** The continuation of the keel or central spine up the line of the bow. The bow of the boat.

**STOCKS** A long straight beam of timber on which the keel is supported during building.

**STRAKE** The run of plank from stem to stern. It may be made from several pieces scarfed together.

**THWARTS** Seats on which the oarsmen sit. Timbers the internal 'ribs'of a boat.

**TRANSOM STERN** A transverse, flat, or 'fish-tail' stern as opposed to a pointed end stern.

**'THE TURN'** The short curved section of keel below the stem, also called the 'forefoot'.

**'WEE-HILL'** A fishing area or 'mark' which was located from the sea by waiting till a certain small hill appeared between two larger ones inland from Culdaff.

**WEARING** Local Donegal name for a narrow plank running the length of the inside of the boat below the gunwale. The thwarts were placed on the wearing. Also called a 'Bearer'.

# GAELIC TERMS

**Gaelic terms used in Inishboffin for the parts of the Drontheim**

| | |
|---|---|
| AFT BEAM | *Táibhte Deireadh* |
| AFT MANSAIL | *Seól Deireadh* |
| APRON | *Naprún* |
| BALLAST | *Balláiste* |
| BEAM OAR | *Táibhte Mór* |
| BEAM | *Tuataigh* |
| BECKIT | *Beoradh* |
| BOW OAR | *(Táibhte) Tosaigh* |
| BOW | *Tosaigh* |
| FORE MAINSAIL | *Seól Tosaigh* |
| HALLIARD | *Lainéir* |
| HELM | *Láimhe / Máide Stiúreadh* |
| KNEES | *Glúine* |
| LOOSE BEAM | *Táibhte Scaoilte* |
| MAST | *Crann* |
| OAR | *Máide Rámha* |
| PINS | *Pionnaí Iomradh* |
| PLANKS | *Cláiridh / Cláirí* |
| ROWTH | *Leap Iomradh* |
| RUDDER | *Stúir* |
| SHEET | *Scód* |
| SHOE | *Steip* |
| STAY | *Stróite* |
| TIMBERS | *Cais Adhmáid* |

# SCOTS - GAELIC TERMS

Scots-Gaelic terms used on Islay for the parts of the
*Sgoth Eirreanach*

| | | | |
|---|---|---|---|
| Aft beam | *Tobhta dheiridh* | Oar | *Ràmh* |
| Apron | *Aparan* | Oar-blade | *Dòirneag* |
| Bailer-dish | *Taoman* | Plank | *Strac or Bòrd-clàr* |
| Beam or seat | *Tobhta* | Quarter | *Sliasaid* |
| Black squalls | *Fuaraidh dhubha* | Round stern | *Deireadh-cuaiche* |
| Breast-hook | *Gobhlan* | Rowth | *Clabhatan* |
| Bung | *Spiocaid* | Rudder | *Stiùir* |
| Cod | *Trosc* | Rudder lock | *Ghlas a'stiùir* |
| Fish-oil lamp | *Cruisgean* | Rudder-irons | *Iarunn-stiùireach* |
| Forward -beam | *Tobhta thoisich* | Saddle | *Dialedh* |
| Frame or rib | *Aisean* | Sail | *Aodach* |
| Gaff | *Cleibe* | Sandstroke | *Fliuch-bhòrd* |
| Gunwale | *Beul stoc* | Shoulder | *Gualainn* |
| Head-sail | *Ceann aodach* | Side- knee or "oxter" | *Asgall* |
| Keel | *Druim* | Sprit | *Spreòd* |
| Kelp or tangle | *Slat-mhara* | Sprit-sail | *Seòl-spreòid* |
| Knee, or knee-heads | *Ceann tobhta* | Stay | *Stadh* |
| Leather lure (for cod) | *Cliobain* | Stenlock (coalfish) | *Ugsa* |
| Lee-side | *Taobh leis* | String of fish | *Gad éisg* |
| Loose or lifting beam | *Tobhta togalaich* | Thole- pin | *Putag* |
| Lugsail yard | *Slat-shiùil* | Tiller | *Ailm* |
| Mast beam | *Tobhta chroinn* | Wearing or bearer for beams | *Giùlanair* |
| Mast lock or clasp | *Ghlas a'chroinn* | Weather-side | *Taobh an fhuaraidh* |
| Mast | *Crann* | | |

# A WORD OF THANKS

A gain to … the late Dan Lafferty of Moville who first told me about the drontheims so long ago now. Packie 'Liza' Doherty of Glengad who gave me the gift of the first photograph and who introduced me to Barney McKeeny who sang me a song about drontheims. The McDonald brothers of the boatyard. Des, Charlie and Marie McCann of Strove. Frank 'the Post' McLaughlin. James McLaughlin for the lighthouse journal. James Canavan, Mick Kelly, Hugh Tinney, Norris Kane, Mrs. Anne Loane Ballinamallard, Dan McLaughlin of Coleraine and the many other who generously gave me photographs. Ken Doherty of Newbuildings. Jimmy Ferry, Pat Coll, Sean O'Brien and the fishermen of Inishboffin. Bernard Barr and Gerard Diver who took me sailing in the new drontheims and John 'Jack' McLaughlin who entertained me with his stories.

My thanks also to those who led me from Sligo to Islay for their part of the story:

The McCanns of Moneygold. George, Peter and Paddy Gallagher and Vincent O'Donnell of Inver. Sean O'hEochaigh of Gortahork. Harry Madill for all about Portstewart and his help for the whole book. Sammy Gault, Bertie McKay and Sammy Wilkinson who told me lots of their great stories along the Causeway coast. Loughie McQuilkin and Danny Hannaway of Rathlin Island. Robin Ruddock of Portrush and Arthur McElnay of Moira. Jim and Donalda McFarlane and Joanne McKinnon of Islay.

Michael McCaughan of the Ulster Folk and Transport Museum, Cultra for his help and permission to quote from his writings. Kenneth Anderson who arranged permission to reproduce photographs from the Museum's collection. Also the National Library, Dublin and the Ulster Museum, Belfast for permission to use photographs from their collections. Harry Weir of Monaghan for his work with many of the old photographs.

Kevin McLaverty, formerly of the National Fishery School, Greencastle, for his magnificent technical description, lines and sail plans of the drontheim, and for his wit and infectious love of wooden boats. Joe Lynch of Cullmore who again made the whole thing possible. Claire Mulhall and Charlie Cavanagh of the Greencastle Development Association. Paul and Ciarán Rowe for putting it all patiently together.

And those now dead whom I was fortunate to meet in time… Barney McKenny of Glengad, Danny Sullivan, Liam McCormick, Hugh McCann and Bob Cavanagh of Strove and Tommy Cecil of Rathlin.

Dónal MacPolin, Dublin, June 1999

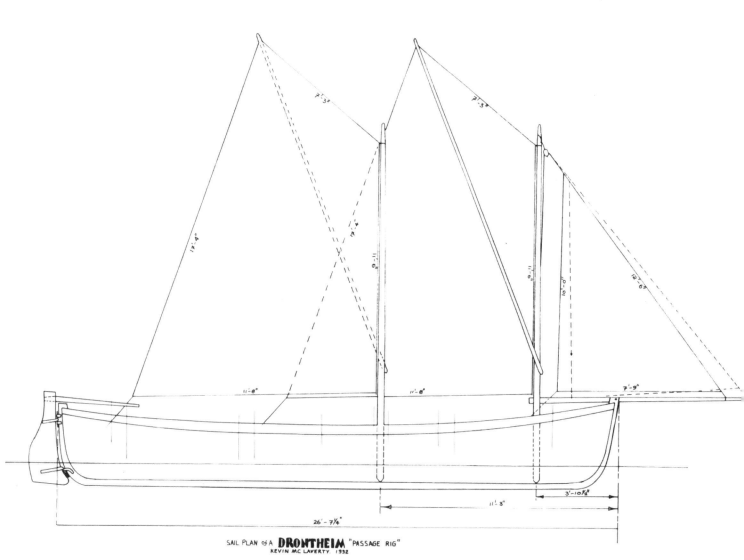

SAIL PLAN of A **DRONTHEIM** "PASSAGE RIG"
KEVIN MC LAVERTY. 1992

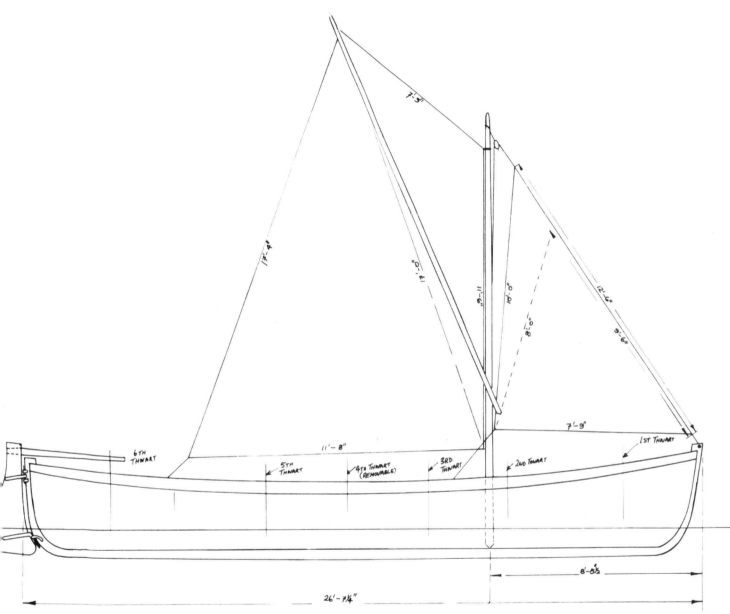

SAIL PLAN of A **DRONTHEIM** "WORKING RIG"

KEVIN MC LAVERTY. 1992